TERRORISM, HOT SPOTS AND CONFLICT-RELATED ISSUES

THE DEATH OF OSAMA BIN LADEN AND RELATED OPERATIONS

TERRORISM, HOT SPOTS AND CONFLICT-RELATED ISSUES

Additional books in this series can be found on Nova's website under the Series tab.

Additional E-books in this series can be found on Nova's website under the E-book tab.

DEFENSE, SECURITY AND STRATEGIES

Additional books in this series can be found on Nova's website under the Series tab.

Additional E-books in this series can be found on Nova's website under the E-book tab.

TERRORISM, HOT SPOTS AND CONFLICT-RELATED ISSUES

THE DEATH OF OSAMA BIN LADEN AND RELATED OPERATIONS

RAYMOND V. DONAHUE
EDITOR

Nova Science Publishers, Inc.
New York

Copyright © 2011 by Nova Science Publishers, Inc.

All rights reserved. No part of this book may be reproduced, stored in a retrieval system or transmitted in any form or by any means: electronic, electrostatic, magnetic, tape, mechanical photocopying, recording or otherwise without the written permission of the Publisher.

For permission to use material from this book please contact us:
Telephone 631-231-7269; Fax 631-231-8175
Web Site: http://www.novapublishers.com

NOTICE TO THE READER

The Publisher has taken reasonable care in the preparation of this book, but makes no expressed or implied warranty of any kind and assumes no responsibility for any errors or omissions. No liability is assumed for incidental or consequential damages in connection with or arising out of information contained in this book. The Publisher shall not be liable for any special, consequential, or exemplary damages resulting, in whole or in part, from the readers' use of, or reliance upon, this material. Any parts of this book based on government reports are so indicated and copyright is claimed for those parts to the extent applicable to compilations of such works.

Independent verification should be sought for any data, advice or recommendations contained in this book. In addition, no responsibility is assumed by the publisher for any injury and/or damage to persons or property arising from any methods, products, instructions, ideas or otherwise contained in this publication.

This publication is designed to provide accurate and authoritative information with regard to the subject matter covered herein. It is sold with the clear understanding that the Publisher is not engaged in rendering legal or any other professional services. If legal or any other expert assistance is required, the services of a competent person should be sought. FROM A DECLARATION OF PARTICIPANTS JOINTLY ADOPTED BY A COMMITTEE OF THE AMERICAN BAR ASSOCIATION AND A COMMITTEE OF PUBLISHERS.

Additional color graphics may be available in the e-book version of this book.

Library of Congress Cataloging-in-Publication Data

The death of Osama bin Laden and related operations / editor, Raymond V. Donahue.
 p. cm.
 Includes index.
 ISBN 978-1-61470-479-9 (hardcover)
 1. Bin Laden, Osama, 1957-2011. 2. Qaida (Organization) 3. Terrorism--United States--Prevention. 4. National security--United States. I. Donahue, Raymond V.
 HV6432.D4313 2011
 363.325'160973--dc23
                              2011024322

Published by Nova Science Publishers, Inc. † New York

CONTENTS

Preface		vii
Chapter 1	Osama bin Laden's Death: Implications and Considerations *John Rollins*	1
Chapter 2	Al Qaeda and Affiliates: Historical Perspective, Global Presence and Implications for U.S. Policy *John Rollins*	33
Chapter 3	U.S. Special Operations Forces (SOF): Background and Issues for Congress *Andrew Feickert and Thomas K. Livingston*	81
Chapter 4	Navy Irregular Warfare and Counterterrorism Operations: Background and Issues for Congress *Ronald O'Rourke*	97
Chapter 5	Sensitive Covert Action Notifications: Oversight Options for Congress *Alfred Cumming*	131
Index		143

PREFACE

The May 1st, 2011 killing of Osama bin Laden by U.S. forces in Pakistan has led to a range of views about near-and long-term security and foreign policy implications for the United States. Experts have a range of views about the killing of Osama bin Laden. Some consider his death to be a largely symbolic event, while others believe it marks a significant achievement in U.S. counterterrorism efforts. The degree to which Osama bin Laden's death will affect Al Qaeda and how the U.S. responds to this event may shape the future of many U.S. national security activities. This book addresses the implications and possible considerations for Congress related to the U.S. killing of bin Laden including military considerations, implications for Pakistan and Afghanistan, and U.S. security interests and foreign policy considerations among others

Chapter 1- Individuals suggesting that the death of Osama bin Laden (OBL) lacks great significance argue that U.S. and allied actions had eroded OBL's ability to provide direction and support to Al Qaeda (AQ). For these analysts, OBL's influence declined following the U.S. invasion of Afghanistan to a point where prior to his death he was the figurehead of an ideological movement. This argument reasons that a shift of terrorist capability has occurred away from the core of AQ to affiliated organizations. Still others argue that OBL pursued a strategy of developing the AQ organization into an ideological movement thus making it more difficult to defeat. They contend that, even if OBL were no longer involved in the decision-making apparatus of AQ, his role as the inspirational leader of the organization was far more important than any operational advice he might offer. As such, his death may not negatively affect the actions of the ideological adherents of AQ and as a martyr he may attract and inspire a greater number of followers.

Chapter 2- Al Qaeda (AQ) has evolved into a significantly different terrorist organization than the one that perpetrated the September 11, 2001, attacks. At the time, Al Qaeda was composed mostly of a core cadre of veterans of the Afghan insurgency against the Soviet Union, with a centralized leadership structure made up mostly of Egyptians. Most of the organization's plots either emanated from the top or were approved by the leadership. Some analysts describe pre-9/11 Al Qaeda as akin to a corporation, with Osama Bin Laden acting as an agile Chief Executive Officer issuing orders and soliciting ideas from subordinates.

Chapter 3- Special Operations Forces (SOF) play a significant role in U.S. military operations, and the Administration has given U.S. SOF greater responsibility for planning and conducting worldwide counterterrorism operations. U.S. Special Operations Command (USSOCOM) has close to 60,000 active duty, National Guard, and reserve personnel from all four services and Department of Defense (DOD) civilians assigned to its headquarters, its four components, and one sub-unified command. The 2010 Quadrennial Defense Review (QDR) directs increases in SOF force structure, particularly in terms of increasing enabling units and rotary and fixed-wing SOF aviation assets and units. USSOCOM Commander, Admiral Eric T. Olson, in commenting on the current state of the forces under his command, noted that since September 11, 2001, USSOCOM manpower has nearly doubled, the budget nearly tripled, and overseas deployments have quadrupled; because of this high level of demand, the admiral added, SOF is beginning to show some "fraying around the edges" and one potential way to combat this is by finding ways to get SOF "more time at home." Admiral Olson also noted the effectiveness of Section 1208 authority, which provides funds for SOF to train and equip regular and irregular indigenous forces to conduct counterterrorism operations.

Chapter 4- The Navy for several years has carried out a variety of irregular warfare (IW) and counterterrorism (CT) activities, and has taken some steps in recent years to strengthen its ability to conduct such activities. Among the most readily visible of the Navy's current IW operations are those being carried out by Navy sailors serving ashore in Afghanistan and Iraq. Many of the Navy's contributions to IW operations around the world are made by Navy individual augmentees (IAs)—individual Navy sailors assigned to various DOD operations.

Chapter 5- Legislation enacted in 1980 gave the executive branch authority to limit advance notification of especially sensitive covert actions to eight Members of Congress—the "Gang of Eight"—when the President determines that it is essential to limit prior notice in order to meet extraordinary circumstances affecting U.S. vital interests. In such cases, the executive branch is permitted by statute to limit notification to the chairmen and ranking minority members of the two congressional intelligence committees, the Speaker and minority leader of the House, and Senate majority and minority leaders, rather than to notify the full intelligence committees, as is required in cases involving covert actions determined to be less sensitive.

In: The Death of Osama bin Laden ...
Editor: Raymond V. Donahue

ISBN: 978-1-61470-479-9
© 2011 Nova Science Publishers, Inc.

Chapter 1

OSAMA BIN LADEN'S DEATH: IMPLICATIONS AND CONSIDERATIONS[*]

John Rollins

SUMMARY

The May 1, 2011 killing of Osama bin Laden (OBL) by U.S. forces in Pakistan has led to a range of views about near- and long-term security and foreign policy implications for the United States. Experts have a range of views about the killing of OBL. Some consider his death to be a largely symbolic event, while others believe it marks a significant achievement in U.S. counterterrorism efforts. Individuals suggesting that his death lacks great significance argue that U.S. and allied actions had eroded OBL's ability to provide direction and support to Al Qaeda (AQ). For these analysts, OBL's influence declined following the U.S. invasion of Afghanistan to a point where prior to his death he was the figurehead of an ideological movement. This argument reasons that a shift of terrorist capability has occurred away from the core of AQ to affiliated organizations. Still others argue that OBL pursued a strategy of developing the AQ organization into an ideological movement thus making it more difficult to defeat. They contend that, even if OBL were no longer involved in the decision-making apparatus of AQ, his role as the inspirational leader of the organization was far more important than

---

[*] This is an edited, reformatted and augmented version of a Congressional Research Service publication, May 5, 2011.

any operational advice he might offer. As such, his death may not negatively affect the actions of the ideological adherents of AQ and as a martyr he may attract and inspire a greater number of followers.

Individuals suggesting that his death is a major turning point in U.S. counterterrorism efforts contend that OBL remained an active participant in setting a direction for the strategy and operations of AQ and its affiliates. In addition to disrupting AQ's organizational activities some believe his death may serve as a defining moment for the post 9/11 global counterterrorism campaign as current and potential terrorists, other governments, and entities that wish to threaten U.S. interests will take note of the U.S. success in achieving a long-held security goal. The death of OBL may have near and long-term implications for AQ and U.S. security strategies and policies.

The degree to which OBL's death will affect AQ and how the U.S. responds to this event may shape the future of many U.S. national security activities. Implications and possible considerations for Congress related to the U.S. killing of OBL in Pakistan are addressed in this report. As applicable, questions related to the incident and U.S. policy implications are also offered. They address:

- Implications for AQ (core, global affiliates, and unaffiliated adherents)
- Congressional Notification
- Legal Considerations
- National Security Considerations and Implications for the Homeland
- Military Considerations
- Implications for Pakistan and Afghanistan
- Implications for U.S. Security Interests and Foreign Policy Considerations

The death of OBL is multi-faceted topic with information emerging frequently that adds perspective and context to many of the issues discussed in this report. This report is based on open-source information and will be updated as necessary.

IMPLICATIONS OF THE DEATH OF OSAMA BIN LADEN

Issues and questions related to the killing of Osama bin Laden (OBL) are multifaceted and may have operational, regional, and policy implications. Operational policy issues include congressional notification, legal considerations, and current and future military activities.

Congressional Notification[1]

The chairmen of the House and Senate intelligence committees have stated that they were briefed on OBL's whereabouts during the past few months including, according to Representative Mike Rogers, Chairman of the House Intelligence Committee, some details regarding the Abbottabad compound. The Senate Majority Leader, Senator Harry Reid, has also indicated that he had been briefed on the plans to confirm OBL's location and take action. Chariman Rogers indicated that the entire "Gang of Eight" had been briefed on the plans although not all were briefed at the same time. The Gang of Eight refers to the eight Members of Congress (the Speaker, House Minority Leader, the Senate Majority and Minority Leaders, and the chairmen and ranking members of the two intelligence committees) who, by statute, must be advised of Presidential Findings of covert actions (along with other members of the congressional leadership as may be included by the President).[2] A finding is an official determination by the President that a specific covert action is in the national interest.[3] A covert action is an activity to influence political, economic, or military conditions abroad where the role of the U.S. will not be apparent or acknowledged publicly.[4] In a PBS News Hour interview on May 3, CIA Director Leon Panetta stated, "this was what's called a 'Title 50' operation, which is a covert operation, and it comes directly from the President of the United States who made the decision to conduct this operation in a covert way." He added that, consistent with Title 50, he commanded the mission but it was carried out by Vice Admiral William McRaven, the commander of the Joint Special Operations Command.

Possible Questions

Notwithstanding the notification process that was carried out with this particular operation, other considerations and questions may still emerge. For example,

- In retrospect, was congressional notification overly restrictive? When was the written Presidential Finding (required by 50 USC 413b(a)(1)) reported to the several members of the Gang of Eight? Has the written Finding now been shared with all members of the two intelligence committees?
- Did the operation necessarily constitute a cover action? Could it have been considered a traditional military activity? Was the role of the CIA Director essential to carrying out the operation? Could it have

been carried out by the Secretary of Defense? Other than the role of Director Panetta what was the contribution of CIA officials to carrying out the raid?
- Should there be statutory provisions requiring that the Armed Services committees (or their respective leaderships) be advised of activities such as the Abbottabad raid?

Legal Considerations[5]

The death of OBL appears to have little, if any, immediate consequence for the legal framework governing the conflict with Al Qaeda (AQ) and its affiliates. Shortly after the attacks of September 11, 2001, Congress passed the Authorization to Use Military Force (AUMF, P.L. 107- 40), which authorized the President:

> to use all necessary and appropriate force against those nations, organizations, or persons he determines planned, authorized, committed, or aided the terrorist attacks that occurred on September 11, 2001, or harbored such organizations or persons, in order to prevent any future acts of international terrorism against the United States by such nations, organizations or persons.

By conferring authority "to use all necessary and appropriate force" against entities involved in the 9/11 attacks, the AUMF is understood to not only authorize the use of force against such groups, but also to permit other fundamental incidents to the waging of war, including the detention of captured enemy belligerents to prevent their return to hostilities.[6] Pursuant to this authority, the United States has engaged in military operations against AQ, the Taliban, and associated forces located in Afghanistan and other locations, and it has detained belligerents captured in these operations at the U.S. Naval Station at Guantanamo Bay, Cuba, and other locations.

Due to OBL's position in AQ's command structure, along with his role in the 9/11 attacks, there appears to be clear consensus that he constituted a legitimate target under the AUMF at the time of his death. Additionally, the AUMF does not restrict the exercise of the authority it confers to a particular geographic location. Accordingly, at least for purposes of domestic law,[7] the fact that OBL was killed outside of Afghanistan, where U.S. operations against AQ have primarily occurred, does not appear to affect the lawfulness of his targeting.[8]

While OBL was a legitimate target under the AUMF, his death does not result in the termination of the authority conferred by the act. The AUMF authorizes the use of force against all "nations, organizations, or persons" determined to have been involved in the 9/11 attacks. OBL's demise would not appear to affect the AUMF's continued application to AQ and any other entity believed to have "planned, authorized, committed, or aided" the 9/11 attacks or harbored such persons or groups, so as to prevent any future terrorist attacks by such entities against the United States. Even though OBL's death does not have the immediate legal consequence of modifying the authority conferred by the AUMF, it is nonetheless possible that his demise may inform future deliberations by policymakers as to whether to alter the legal framework governing U.S. policy towards AQ and its affiliates.[9]

Military Considerations[10]

The successful U.S. military operation against OBL carries with it possible military implications for the future. In terms of U.S. adversaries, it can be argued that the operation can serve as a powerful deterrent to both current and aspiring terrorist leaders. The search for OBL took almost a decade to develop and execute, spanned two very different Administrations with the operation conducted in a sovereign nation, apparently without their knowledge or consent, against a target that was considered by some analysts as well hidden and protected. Some contend that this sends the message that no matter how long it takes and how difficult the circumstances, the U.S. will ultimately kill or capture senior terrorist leadership. While this could convey a potential deterrence message, it also suggests that in the future, more concerted measures will need to be taken by terrorist organizations to protect their leadership, which could make military operations against them more difficult.

Another implication is that the U.S. military has demonstrated a highly refined and sophisticated ability to locate, track, and interdict high value targets anywhere in the world. While this capability has been associated with counterterrorism efforts, there are also implications for counter weapons of mass destruction (WMD) efforts as well as other national security-related efforts. These capabilities could also affect physical security planning and measures of adversarial countries or non-state actors that either aspire to or possess WMDs.

Command and Control of the Operation

During the President's May 1, 2011 address to the nation about the killing of Osama OBL, he noted that, "and so shortly after taking office, I directed Leon Panetta, the director of the CIA, to make the killing or capture of Osama bin Laden the top priority of our war against Al Qaeda."[11] During later briefings, it was revealed that the operation was carried out by U.S. Navy SEALs from the U.S. Special Operations Command. These and other briefings seem to suggest that the military operation to kill OBL was commanded by the CIA as opposed to the more traditional military chain of command. While this would not be unprecedented, it can be considered unusual and Congress might wish to clarify the operation's actual chain of command with the Administration. There could also be concerns that this arrangement might have been a less than optimal arrangement and that there could have been undo friction between the CIA and the Department of Defense (DoD), resulting in a negative impact on mission planning, resourcing, and execution. On the other hand, if this arrangement proved to be highly successful and relatively problem-free, the CIA/military command arrangement might serve as a model for future operations of a similar nature.

Possible Questions

Reports that the CIA commanded the operation, suggest a number of considerations that might merit further examination. For example:

- Why was this particular command arrangement chosen over a more traditional CIA commanded/CIA conducted operation or a military commanded/ military conducted operation?
- Was there a legal basis for this command arrangement or were special authorities or arrangements required?
- If the command arrangment is seen as a model, do current U.S. laws and policies support this type of arrangement, to include legal provisions pertaining to congressional notification and oversight?

AL QAEDA, REGIONAL, AND COUNTRY IMPLICATIONS

The killing of OBL nearly ten years after the September 11, 2001 terrorist attacks on the United States poses many questions about the continuing destructive capabilities of AQ, the effects on regional affiliates and U.S. policy implications in Pakistan and Afghanistan.

Implications for AQ, Affiliates, and Unaffiliated Adherents[12]

Ascertaining the near- and long-term implications of OBL's death on AQ operations will be the subject of much analysis and debate for U.S. policymakers. Those implications may differ for core AQ leaders,[13] their global affiliates,[14] and non-affiliated ideological adherents[15] of AQ around the world. In describing the significance of OBL's role in AQ government leaders and analysts offer a variety of perspectives. Some argue that OBL's role in AQ at the time of his death was largely inspirational as his ability to communicate with followers and offer strategic and operational guidance and support had increasingly been degraded since the U.S. invasion of Afghanistan. Others argue that OBL remained an active participant in both the strategic direction and operational activities of all aspects of the AQ movement.[16] With the death of OBL and U.S. seizure of documents and electronic data devices from his compound some analysts suggest further disruption to global AQ related activities may be expected, including infighting between the remaining leaders of core AQ, lack of cohesion in and between the affiliated organizations, and fewer individuals recruited or radicalized to support AQ's goals. Should these events materialize, U.S. security agencies and international partners may have an opportunity to exploit vulnerabilities with the goal of hastening the demise of AQ and its affiliated organizations. However, some analysts may argue that the regional global affiliates are the least likely AQ entity to be affected by OBL's death.

In December 2010, National Counterterrorism Center (NCTC) Director Michael Leiter offered the following assessment of the relationship between core AQ and its affiliates:

> affiliates have no longer simply relied upon their linkages to al-Qaida senior leadership in Pakistan but they have in fact emerged more as self-sustaining, independent movements and organizations. Now, they still have important tentacles back to al-Qaida senior leadership—I don't want to downplay that—but in many ways, especially in the case of al-Qaida and the Arabian Peninsula, operate with a greater level of independence. And, frankly, they operate at a different pace and with a different level of complexity than does al-Qaida senior leadership, and that has complicated our task significantly.[17]

Implications of OBL's Death on AQ's Global Affiliates[18]

The potential impact of OBL's death on AQ's global affiliates remains uncertain, in part because the specific operational ties between regional groups and core AQ elements in Afghanistan and Pakistan are not well understood outside of the intelligence community. In many instances, both operational and ideological ties appear to be limited, and most regional affiliates appear to have operated largely autonomously. The most common reported type of linkage between the core and global affiliates has taken the form of pledges of ideological fealty by regional affiliates to OBL, along with mutual statements of support for shared goals. A second, more opaque link between the core and the global affiliates are reported periodic exchanges for strategic planning between the core and affiliates and, in some cases, the exchange of financing or the deployment of technical experts to the affiliates by the core group.

To the extent that the killing of OBL disrupts the organizational cohesion of the core group, these pledges and apparently limited exchanges may decline in frequency and scope. That possibility may be magnified if post-OBL leadership succession within the core group is contested—as implied by some analyses suggesting that Ayman al Zawahiri may be viewed unfavorably, for various reasons, by some core group elements. Such ties may also decline if intelligence gleaned from the operation targeting OBL spurs follow-on operations resulting in core group leadership killings, arrests, or other disruptions.

Weakened core-regional ties may also lead global affiliates to become even more operationally and autonomous and diverse, and potentially more politically differentiated as well. Global affiliates may see a need to rely more on local financial, human, and technical resources and may focus increased attention on local political grievances and social dynamics. Alternatively, in the short term, affiliates may re-orient their current local operations to respond to OBL's death, for instance, by moving up the timeline for planned attacks or by changing the terms of on-going hostage negotiations that would have transnational implications. Another possibility is that one or more affiliates might eclipse or replace the core Afghanistan-Pakistan based leadership, whether intentionally or due to the course of events.

The success of the U.S. operation targeting OBL may also motivate an increased U.S. operational emphasis on targeting key leaders of regional groups, especially if post-OBL field assessments of the core group indicate that its operational capacity has been degraded and if, as a result, the perceived threat posed by global affiliates takes on relatively greater importance. Increasing autonomy and differentiation among regional affiliates may, however, make tracking and targeting these groups and their members more difficult, as operations to do so may require increasingly focused, specialized, and dedicated expertise and human and intelligence assets. If global affiliates become more insular, this could prompt a decline in communications and resource exchanges between the core group and global affiliates, and thus a relative decline in opportunities to exploit or interdict these connections.

The findings from future assessments of core and affiliated AQ capabilities may have significant global policy implications for the United States. While the consequences of OBL's death are unknown at present, U.S. actions leading up to and after his death may have implications for numerous U.S. policy issues.

Pakistan[19]

OBL was located and killed in the mid-sized Pakistani city of Abbottabad, a military cantonment in the northwest Khyber Pakhtunkhwa province, in a compound one-half mile from the country's premier military academy.[20] The location and circumstances of OBL's killing have exacerbated Washington's long-held doubts about Pakistan's commitment to ostensibly shared goals of defeating religious extremism, and may jeopardize future U.S. assistance to Pakistan.[21] The news of OBL's whereabouts led to almost immediate questioning of Pakistan's role and potential complicity in his refuge; a senior Administration official expressed being "very concerned" that OBL was inside Pakistan and indicated that the U.S. government would carefully question Islamabad in this regard. President Obama's chief counterterrorism advisor, John Brennan, told reporters it was "inconceivable that Osama bin Laden did not have a support system" in Pakistan.[22]

The development has made much more acute already existing doubts about Pakistan's role as a U.S. ally in counterterrorism (CT) efforts. In the representative words of one senior, U.S.-based nongovernmental expert on AQ and OBL,

> It stretches credulity to think that a mansion of that scale could have been built and occupied by OBL for six years without its coming to the attention of anyone in the Pakistani Army. The initial circumstantial evidence suggests that the opposite is more likely—that OBL was effectively being housed under Pakistani state control. ... Perhaps the circumstantial evidence in the OBL case is misleading; only a transparent, thorough investigation by Pakistani authorities into how such a fugitive could have lived so long under the military's nose without detection would establish otherwise. That sort of transparent investigation is unlikely to take place.[23]

Given this, contends another leading analyst, some Americans feel that they have seen

> their worst suspicions confirmed by the fact that Osama bin Laden lived in a large, well-protected compound right under the Pakistani military's nose. Either Pakistan's intelligence service is terribly incompetent, fatally compromised, or both, raising questions about its utility as a partner.[24]

Thus, for a wide array of observers, the outcome of the years-long hunt for OBL leaves only two realistic conclusions: either Pakistani officials were at some level complicit in hiding the fugitive, or the country's military and intelligence services were exceedingly incompetent in their search for top AQ leaders. In either case, after many years of claims by senior Pakistani officials—both civilian and military—that most-wanted extremist figures were finding no refuge in their country, Pakistan's credibility has suffered a serious blow.[25]

Although relatively subdued in their responses, Pakistani leaders welcomed the news of OBL's death as a major victory in the battle against terrorism.[26] Pakistani President Asif Zardari penned a May 2, 2011, opinion piece in which he claimed for his country partial credit for the elimination of OBL, reiterated the suffering and loss of life Pakistan has endured in combating terrorism, and called media suggestions that Pakistan has lacked determination or sincerity in this effort "baseless speculation," declaring, "Pakistan has never been and never will be the hotbed of fanaticism that is often described by the media."[27] Such claims, already considered dubious, are now widely viewed as lacking credibility by most independent observers.

Implications for the U.S.-Pakistan "Strategic Partnership"

Pakistan is praised by U.S. leaders for its post-2001 cooperation with U.S.-led CT and counterinsurgency efforts, although long-held doubts exist about Islamabad's commitment to some core U.S. interests. A mixed record on battling Islamist extremism includes ongoing apparent tolerance of Taliban elements operating from Pakistan's territory. In his nationally televised address of May 1, 2011, President Obama stated that OBL had been found hiding "deep within Pakistan," and he reiterated again his longstanding intention to "take action within Pakistan" if OBL was located there. While giving no hint as to the extent of Pakistani cooperation in the specific operation, the President said that, "going forward, it is essential that Pakistan continue to join us in the fight against Al Qaeda and its affiliates."[28]

Subsequently, other top Administration officials have emphasized the need for close cooperation with Pakistan.

These sentiments track well with the view of many independent observers that—despite ample reasons for discouragement and distrust—the United States has no good options other than continuing to engage Pakistan in what one analyst calls "the geostrategic equivalent of a bad marriage."[29] These experts contend that a U.S. disengagement from Pakistan would likely only facilitate greater extremism and anti-American sentiment there, and that a sustained effort to assist in improving Pakistan's political, economic, and security circumstances is the best strategy. There are hopes among some analysts that the circumstances of OBL's death will inspire soul-searching in Pakistani leaders and perhaps more robust cooperation with the United States in the future.[30] At the same time, Pakistan's main international rival, India, is now set to increase its long-existing efforts to convince Washington to more intensely scrutinize its relationship with Islamabad.[31]

Some senior Members of Congress have voiced the opinion that present circumstances call for "more engagement [with Pakistan], not less."[32] Yet Capitol Hill has also been the site of sometimes pointed questioning of the wisdom of continued engagement with a national government that may at some levels have knowledge of OBL's whereabouts, with figures from both major parties expressing disbelief at Pakistan's allegations of ignorance and calling for greater oversight and accountability for future U.S. assistance to Pakistan.[33]

Questions About U.S. Foreign Assistance to Pakistan

Although there is considerable agreement in U.S. government circles that disengaging from Pakistan is an unwise course, intensive congressional scrutiny of U.S. assistance to Pakistan is already underway. In the post 9/11 era, Congress has appropriated more than $20 billion in foreign assistance and military "reimbursements" for Pakistan, placing that country among the top recipients of U.S. financial support over the past decade.[34] The Obama Administration has requested nearly $3 billion in further security- and development-related assistance to Pakistan for FY2012, along with more than $1 billion for continued reimbursements to the Pakistani military.

As the incidence of Islamist militancy spread in recent years, anti-U.S. and anti-Western terrorist plots increasingly were traced to Pakistan-based extremist groups, and the Afghan insurgency continued to benefit from "safe havens" in western Pakistan, many in Congress began to question the efficacy of major aid disbursements to a country that was making little or no progress toward longstanding U.S. goals ostensibly shared by Islamabad. Such questioning sharpened in late 2010 and early 2011, especially with the acrimony surrounding the early 2011 Raymond Davis affair, in which a CIA contractor shot and killed two Pakistani men in Lahore and was imprisoned for seven weeks before his mid-March release.[35]

In the wake of revelations that the world's most-wanted terrorist had apparently been living for years in a comfortable home in a relatively affluent city and only one kilometer away from Pakistan's premier military academy, congressional skepticism about the continuation of large aid disbursements to Pakistan has deepened even further.[36] On May 3, 2011, H.R. 1699, the Pakistan Foreign Aid Accountability Act, was introduced in the House. The Act would prohibit future foreign assistance to Pakistan unless the Secretary of State certifies that the Pakistani government was not complicit in hiding OBL. Depending on the course of Pakistan's future policy statements and levels of cooperation with the United States, Congress may choose to adjust current assistance funding levels. Such funding flows are already hindered by U.S. concerns about corruption and lack of transparency in Pakistan's implementing partners.[37]

Questions About Bilateral Security and Intelligence Cooperation

U.S. government suspicions about some level of official Pakistani complicity in protecting wanted terrorists pre-date the 9/11 attacks. Obama Administration officials have at times been explicit in expressing such suspicions, perhaps more strongly than did their predecessors. The developments of May 1 appear for many to strongly vindicate these kinds of concerns. The U.S. government is now likely to ramp up pressure on Islamabad to locate and capture OBL's deputy, Ayman al-Zawahri, and Taliban leader Mullah Omar, both of whom are widely believed to be in Pakistan.

No intelligence on the May 1 operation was shared with Pakistan; only after the raid were Pakistani leaders briefed on the results.[38] Lead U.S. counterterrorism advisor John Brennan has stated that there is no evidence Pakistani officials knew of OBL's whereabouts, but that the United States is not ruling out the possibility.[39] Unnamed Pakistani intelligence officials initially claimed that the raid was a joint operation "based on intelligence input from" and carried out "primarily" by the ISI, with some going so far as to say the operation could not have succeeded without Pakistani involvement. They later conceded that no Pakistanis participated.[40] Yet some analysts are suspicious of the timing of the operation, noting that Pakistan has a record of producing high-value terrorist suspects at seemingly opportune moments and perhaps "played the Osama card" just as U.S.-Pakistan relations were at an acutely low ebb.[41]

Among the key questions yet to be answered in the wake of OBL's killing is what response the Pakistani government gives to the covert U.S. mission on its territory. The Pakistani military and intelligence services are now under pressure to explain how the mastermind of the 9/11 attacks was able to stay so deep inside Pakistan near a military academy. Whatever the answer—incompetence or complicity—the dynamics provide the U.S. government new leverage in pushing Pakistan to take more positive steps, though some argue that they also point to the limitations of what intelligence cooperation can be expected to achieve. To the extent that official Pakistan is subdued in its criticism or even implicitly accepting of the development, most analysts believe intelligence cooperation can continue and even improve, perhaps with the United States recalibrating incentives and disincentives for Pakistan's security services.[42] Such a course could reverse some of the damage seen in the bilateral intelligence relationship in recent months, especially following the early 2011 Raymond Davis episode (noted above).

Increased bilateral acrimony remains a possibility, however. In what is described as an effort to recover from an initial day of confusion and paralysis, Islamabad stiffened its stand on the May 1 events, with the Foreign Ministry expressing "deep concerns and reservations" about the manner in which the U.S. government carried out the operation "without prior information or authorization" from Islamabad:

> This event of unauthorized unilateral action cannot be taken as a rule. The Government of Pakistan further affirms that such an event shall not serve as a future precedent for any state, including the U.S. Such actions undermine cooperation and may also sometime constitute threat to international peace and security.[43]

Islamabad is in the difficult situation of having to balance a need to maintain appearances of strength and competence with a need to avoid antagonizing the United States, a key partner and foreign aid donor. The Foreign Ministry statement also includes extensive discussion of Pakistan's alleged intelligence prowess—even as related to surveillance in Abbottabad—and of its ability to protect Pakistani territory and airspace from foreign intrusion. While it is an open question whether Pakistan will take an increasingly adversarial position going forward, current signs are that Islamabad remains fundamentally committed to cooperative efforts in combating terrorism and militancy, although perhaps not to the point desired by U.S. officials.[44]

Implications for Existing Anti-American Sentiment in Pakistan

Anti-American sentiments and xenophobic conspiracy theories remain rife among ordinary Pakistanis. Many across the spectrum of Pakistani society express anger at U.S. global foreign policy, in particular when such policy is perceived to be unfriendly or hostile to the Muslim world. Pakistani citizens were already angered by U.S.-launched drone strikes and perceptions of unilateral U.S. intelligence operations on Pakistani territory. Such anger is likely to spike in the wake of an apparently unilateral U.S. commando raid deep inside Pakistan.

To date, the tone and tenor of Pakistani media reporting on OBL's death has been seen as largely positive. The information minister's emphasis on OBL's status as a foreigner was widely reported in a positive light. Yet some outlets have harshly questioned the apparent absence of a Pakistani government role in the operation and a perception that it had permitted the country's sovereignty to be violated. Much anger was expressed that Pakistan's leaders had allowed the country to be embarrassed and shamed. Some high-profile critics of the United States declared that OBL's death removed all justification for a continued U.S. presence in the region. Still, no media outlets are known to have openly expressed sympathy for OBL, and in only a single instance was his death referred to as "martyrdom."[45]

OBL did have a sizeable contingent of supporters in Pakistan, although many or most of these had favorable views rooted more in his embodiment of anti-American resistance than in his violent jihadi methods. Yet the numbers of Pakistanis willing to take to the streets in OBL's honor were quite few; two notable rallies took place immediately following the killing (in Quetta and Karachi), and these were comprised of perhaps 1,000 participants each.[46]

Possible Implications for Pakistan-India Relations

The circumstances of OBL's death could affect the course of relations between Pakistan and its historic rival India. Indian Prime Minister Manmohan Singh called the killing "a significant step forward" and expressed hope that it would represent a decisive blow to AQ and other terrorist groups. The Indian External Affairs Ministry hailed the "historic development and victorious milestone in the global war against forces of terrorism."[47] India's foreign and home ministers both took the opportunity to focus on the new evidence that terrorists find sanctuary in Pakistan, and concerns were raised that reprisal attacks could come in Indian Kashmir. Still, most analysts do not foresee the development as derailing New Delhi's recent decision to reengage a robust peace dialogue with Pakistan, even if such dialogue is made more complicated by May 1's events.[48]

At the same time, however, there may be some apprehension in New Delhi that the development could hasten a U.S. withdrawal from Afghanistan in ways that could be harmful to India's foreign policy interests. India is averse to seeing a Kabul government too friendly with Islamabad in the future and has a keen interest in precluding the resurgence of Islamist extremist groups in Afghanistan, which it fears could be the case if the Pakistani military has excessive influence on the anti-Taliban campaign's endgame.[49] New Delhi also sees the discovery of OBL in Pakistan as an opportunity to more energetically press its demands that Islamabad extradite the alleged perpetrators of the 2008 Mumbai terrorist attack, Lashkar-e-Taiba figures believed to be in Pakistan, as well as other most-wanted anti-India terrorists such as Dawood Ibrahim.[50]

Possible Implications for Pakistan-Afghanistan Relations

The ongoing insurgency in Afghanistan and its connection to developments in Pakistan remain matters of serious concern to U.S. policy makers. NATO remains reliant upon logistical routes through Pakistan to supply its forces in Afghanistan, and these landlines of communication regularly come under attack by militants. It is widely held that success in Afghanistan cannot come without the close engagement and cooperation of Pakistan, and that the key to stabilizing Afghanistan is to improve the longstanding animosity between Islamabad and Kabul.

Pakistan's relations with its western neighbor have warmed in the past year, but remain tense given historic differences over Pashtun nationalism and contending accusations about cross-border militancy and terrorism. Afghan officials have stated flatly that Pakistan's security services "should have known" about OBL's whereabouts.[51] Afghan President Karzai claimed that OBL's killing inside Pakistan vindicated his government's opposition to increased U.S.-military operations in Afghanistan, saying the "war on terror" should focus on "the safe havens of terrorism outside Afghanistan." Some Afghan officials are wary that OBL's death would provide justification for a "premature" U.S. disengagement from the region.[52]

At the same time, OBL's death could ease Pakistan-Afghanistan tensions if it leads Islamabad to reevaluate its more direct efforts to shape the outcome of Afghan political reconciliation. There has been concern in Washington DC and other Western capitals that Pakistan had in 2010 begun to take a more aggressive and even unilateralist approach to shaping the course of peace negotiations and potential reconciliation in Afghanistan. This was seen in its arrests of certain Taliban figures in Pakistan who were pursuing reconciliation with the Karzai government and in Islamabad's purported protection of the hard line insurgent faction of Jalaluddin Haqqani in North Waziristan.

Issues in Pakistan's Domestic Setting

OBL's demise could have significant political and security ramifications for Pakistan. Islamabad's already fragile civilian government—widely viewed as unable to govern effectively and overwhelmed with mere survival—will see its standing further complicated. In the days immediately following the death, a dearth of official Pakistani responses—in particular from its military and intelligence services—was taken as an indication of national shock and embarrassment.[53] Early official government statements emphasized U.S. action and refrained from portraying a Pakistani role, possibly in an effort to avoid antagonizing extremist organizations already promising revenge attacks, and also to direct public anger away from the federal government and toward the perceived infringement of Pakistani sovereignty by a foreign power.[54]

With official Pakistani acknowledgement that the raid was a wholly U.S. operation and that Pakistani leaders had not been consulted beforehand, the government and security services, alike, were placed in the awkward position of having to defend against new accusations that they are unable to stand up to foreign powers and protect Pakistani territory and interests.[55] Such accusations are especially stinging in the wake of the Raymond Davis imbroglio and an increasingly unpopular U.S.-led drone campaign in western Pakistan. This means that even the relatively well-respected Pakistan army is coming under intense criticism for either knowing of OBL's whereabouts or not, a significant embarrassment for them in either case.[56]

Pakistan is also bracing for an expected wave of revenge attacks from AQ and its numerous affiliates based in the country. A statement from a Tehrik-e-Taliban Pakistan ("Pakistani Taliban") spokesman vowed retaliation for OBL's killing, saying, "President Zardari and the army will be our first targets, America will be our second target." Intelligence agencies reportedly have warned that Pakistan could see a steep rise in domestic terrorist attacks in the near-term, with U.S. diplomatic missions named as primary targets, along with Pakistani government and military facilities.[57]

Afghanistan[58]

The death of OBL may have profound implications for the U.S. and NATO mission in Afghanistan. Following a strategy review, President Obama, in a major speech on Afghanistan policy at West Point on December 1, 2009, defined the mission in Afghanistan as follows:

> Our overarching goal [in Afghanistan] remains the same: to disrupt, dismantle, and defeat AQ in Afghanistan and Pakistan, and to prevent its capacity to threaten American and our allies in the future.

With OBL now dead, some argue that this overarching goal has now been accomplished, and that U.S. forces can now be withdrawn from Afghanistan. Others argue that AQ's network of operatives and supporters in Afghanistan and Pakistan remains robust, in spite of the loss of its nominal leader. The death of OBL occurred as the Administration was already debating the size and scope of an initial drawdown, to begin in July 2011 as per the West Point speech discussed above, of the 99,000 U.S. forces currently in Afghanistan. Press reports quoting Administration officials say these officials recognize that the death of OBL could increase U.S. public pressure for a more rapid drawdown in Afghanistan than might have been considered before.

Others, reportedly including those in the U.S. military who recommended current policy, believe that the death of OBL is likely to have minimal effect on the threat profile in Afghanistan, and that the U.S.-led mission there would be jeopardized by a rapid withdrawal. Although the stated goal of U.S. policy focuses on eliminating safe haven for terrorist groups, preventing reinfiltration of terrorist groups into Afghanistan is predicated on establishing durable security and capable and effective governance throughout Afghanistan. The death of OBL, and potential weakening of AQ, does not, in and of itself, accomplish these objectives. As noted in Defense Department reports, the most recent of which was released on May 3, 2011, security is being challenged by a confluence of related armed groups whose tactics continue to evolve based on experiences from previous fighting.[59]

Of these groups, AQ has been among the least materially significant to the fighting in Afghanistan, but may pose the greatest regional threat and transnational threat to the United States and its allies. Director of Central Intelligence Leon Panetta said on June 27, 2010, that AQ fighters in Afghanistan itself might number 50-100.[60] NATO/ISAF officials said in October 2010, that AQ cells may be moving back into remote areas of Kunar and Nuristan provinces,[61] particularly in areas vacated by U.S.-led forces. A targeted effort against AQ operatives in those areas in April 2011 killed a leading Saudi AQ operative. Press reports in April 2011 added that some AQ training camps might have been established inside Afghanistan. Top U.S. and NATO commander in Afghanistan, General David Petraeus, said that although the AQ presence in Afghanistan remains small at "less than 100 or so," and in his view, operations to stabilize Afghanistan are necessary to prevent a broader reinfiltration.[62]

There is broad agreement among experts and U.S. officials that the core of the insurgency remains the Taliban movement centered around Mullah Umar, who led the Taliban regime during 1996-2001. Mullah Umar and many of his top advisers remain at large and are reportedly running their insurgency from safe haven in Pakistan. They are believed to be primarily in and around the city of Quetta, according to Afghan officials, thus accounting for the term usually applied to Umar and his aides: "Quetta Shura Taliban" (QST). Some believe that Umar and his inner circle blame their past association with AQ for their loss of power and seek to distance themselves from AQ. Other experts see continuing close association that is likely to continue were the Taliban movement to return to power. Other insurgents, particularly fighters associated with long-time commander Jalaluddin Haqqani and his son Sirajuddin, remain a potentially less reconcilable threat to the Afghan government, and the Haqqani faction has long had close ties to AQ.

It is unclear if internal Taliban debates might be affected by the death of AQ founder OBL. Some within the movement might argue that OBL's removal from the regional picture might lessen international military pressure on all Afghanistan militant groups, and that continued association with AQ carries fewer costs than when OBL was still at large. Others in the Taliban movement might argue that his death leaves AQ weakened and therefore of little value to the Taliban effort. Still others say that the personal relationship between Umar and OBL has become irrelevant now that OBL is dead, and removes this as a factor in continuing to associate with AQ.

Other experts and Administration commentary offer an alternate interpretation of OBL's death. According to some, the death of OBL might facilitate a political solution to the conflict in Afghanistan.[63] Under a "reconciliation" initiative originated by President Karzai in 2009 and generally backed by the United States, there have been informal talks between Afghan officials and those close to or purporting to represent the Taliban movement, or at least parts of it. Some believe that the U.S. killing of OBL, which demonstrates U.S. reach to find and strike Pakistan-based militants directly—

coupled with the pre-existing pressure from the 2009-2011 "surge" of U.S. forces in Afghanistan—could prompt key Taliban leaders to engage in serious settlement negotiations.

Possible Questions

A number of key questions and indicators about U.S. policy in Afghanistan may be considered in the wake of the death of OBL, including:

- How might the Afghan government react to signs of U.S. domestic pressure to accelerate a withdrawal from Afghanistan? Will the Afghan government try to more closely align with other powers, such as China and Russia, if it feels it is about to be "abandoned" by the United States?
- Within Afghanistan, could the perception of an accelerated U.S. drawdown cause some Afghans to give support to the Taliban-led insurgency, believing the insurgency likely to prevail in the absence of U.S. forces? Does the death of OBL make a Taliban role in a future Afghan government more palatable to some Afghans?
- If there is a U.S. decision to accelerate talks with the Taliban or withdraw from Afghanistan, how will key segments of the Afghan population react? For example, will women's groups oppose negotiations with the Taliban, fearing backsliding of their rights if the Taliban is given a share of power? How will the ethnic minorities of the north and west, who fought the Taliban regime during 1996-2001, respond to accelerated negotiations with Taliban figures?
- Discussions about a more rapid transition to Afghan security leadership might hinge on the quality and quantity of the Afghan National Security Forces. How capable are they? If there were a decision on a more rapid transition, to what extent could these Afghan forces be expanded and trained more quickly? What U.S. financial requirements would be involved in a more rapid expansion of the Afghan forces than has been planned to date? How will the Afghan government be able to financially and materially support forces trained to date?

U.S. Strategy and Security Implications

Near- and long-term security and foreign policy considerations may be reassessed with the killing of OBL. The national security community may seek to revise foreign policy and counterterrorism priorities while pursing actions to limit the possible threats to U.S. interests resulting from OBL's death.

National Security Considerations[64]

In the wake of OBL's death, many practitioners and observers have expressed interest in the implications for U.S. national security strategy—whether and to what extent the U.S. Government's prioritization of CT relative to other national security imperatives, the distribution of CT efforts among U.S. Government agencies, and the relative balance of emphasis between CT and other concerns within key U.S. Government agencies, ought to be adjusted. Such decision-making is likely to be shaped in part by assessments of the impact that OBL's death has on the AQ organization and its affiliates, by developments and considerations concerning other key U.S. national security interests, and by the current climate of relatively constrained resources.

Background

The 2010 *National Security Strategy (NSS)* repeatedly underscores the importance of the mission to "disrupt, dismantle and defeat Al Qaeda and its violent extremist affiliates in Afghanistan, Pakistan, and around the world." That mandate has been understood to include a broad range of activities including—according to the *NSS*—protecting the homeland, securing weapons of mass destruction, denying safe havens, and building partnerships around the world.[65]

In addition, there is a generally shared understanding among practitioners that multiple U.S. government agencies share responsibility for the mission to disrupt and defeat VEOs. The *NSS* calls for an "integrated campaign that judiciously applies every tool of American power—both military and civilian." The Department of Defense's (DoD) 2010 *Quadrennial Defense Review (QDR)* recognizes a military role, naming "succeed[ing] in counterinsurgency, stability, and counterterrorism operations" as one of DoD's six key missions.[66] The State Department's *First Quadrennial Diplomacy and Development Review (QDDR),* also released in 2010, stresses that "the threat of terrorism and violent extremism has become more acute and more immediate," and it argues that countering that threat is not exclusively a military responsibility, but rather one shared by multiple agencies.[67] The *NSS, QDR,* and *QDDR* do not prioritize among the goals and objectives they name. While countering violent extremist threats is understood to be important, existing unclassified strategic guidance does not make clear how important that mission is compared to other key missions. Some practitioners suggest that a sense of relative importance generally comes directly from senior leadership—from statements by the President and from guidance issued by the National Security Council (NSC) process (i.e., the tiered system of Interagency Policy Committees, the Deputies Committee, the Principals Committee, and the NSC itself).[68]

Possible Questions

U.S. National Priorities

President Obama has repeatedly stressed the goal of defeating AQ and other VEOs in both written strategic guidance and public speeches. He has further stated that under that rubric he directed, at the beginning of his Administration, that killing or capturing OBL would be the "top priority of our war against AQ", but that the United States would also continue to "disrupt, dismantle and defeat his network."[69] In the wake of the U.S. operation against OBL, President Obama stressed, "his death does not mark the end of our effort."[70] That statement does not, however, indicate whether the overall "defeat" mission will retain the same *de facto* importance relative to other national security priorities or to broader U.S. national interests.

- To what extent might OBL's death prompt a reduction in the relative importance of countering VEOs, compared to other U.S. national security imperatives, and to broader U.S. national interests?

Balance of Responsibilities among Departments and Agencies

In the wake of OBL's demise, the U.S. government may reconsider not only how much effort to apply to countering VEOs, but also what balance of instruments of national power to apply to that effort. That could affect the relative burdens borne by various U.S. agencies in countering VEOs. Key factors—about which assessments are likely to differ—include not only whether the threat has diminished (or grown); but also how and in what ways the threat may have changed qualitatively. A more diffuse, less well-known, more opportunistic, less predictable set of violent extremist networks, for example, could pose different kinds of challenges and require different kinds of approaches to counter it. A further factor is likely to concern how U.S. allies and partners around the world perceive the nature of the terrorist threat in the wake of OBL's death.

While current national-level unclassified guidance—in particular the *NSS*—does not assign roles and responsibilities in any detail, individual agencies, in their own unclassified guidance— including the *QDR* and the *QDDR*—do assign roles and responsibilities to themselves, under the "defeating VEOs" rubric.

Going forward, some may argue, for example, that OBL's death and its expected impact on AQ and its affiliates should signal both a decreased use of large-scale conventional military operations to counter VEOs, and an increased use of precision operations that leverage sophisticated intelligence assets and high-end surgical military capabilities, on the model of the OBL operation.[71]

Others, focusing less on identified terrorist targets and more on the root causes of terrorism, may call for reassessing the efficacy of the mix of U.S. instruments applied to ameliorating conditions that feed recruitment and tacit popular acceptance of VEOs. Such measures include, for example, countering extremist ideology, and partnering with states around the world to help them develop security forces and/or judicial systems well suited for countering violent extremism. In turn, those missions—and others—are typically executed by a combination of efforts by multiple U.S. Government agencies. For example, both DoD and the State Department execute "communications" programs, targeting a range of audiences in various ways, designed to counter violent extremist ideology. A reassessment of the mix of tools might also include re-evaluation of agencies' respective roles.

- To what extent will, and should, OBL's demise trigger a reassessment of the balance of instruments of national power that the U.S. Government commits to countering violent extremism, and of the distribution of roles and responsibilities among U.S. Government agencies appropriate to that balance?

Priorities within Departments and Agencies

In considering refinements to the relative priority of CT, departments and agencies are likely to be steered primarily by guidance from the White House concerning both overall prioritization and the inter-agency distribution of responsibilities. In addition, agencies are likely to conduct their own more detailed internal assessments of the requirements of their respective parts in a potentially refined CT mission, in the context of a resource-constrained environment.

DoD's current unclassified guidance does not prioritize. The 2010 *QDR* names four "priority objectives": "prevail in today's wars; prevent and deter conflict; prepare to defeat adversaries and succeed in a wide range of contingencies; and preserve and enhance the all-volunteer force." Under the "defeat" objective, in turn, the *QDR* describes a range of future challenges, which include "defeating AQ and its allies". Other challenges include responding to natural disasters, prevailing against state adversaries, securing weapons of mass destruction, stabilizing fragile states, protecting U.S. citizens, conducting cyberspace operations, and preventing human suffering—in short, a robust but non-prioritized list. For DoD, the President's guidance in April 2011 to identify $400 billion in additional cuts to the defense budget between now and 2023, and DoD's plans to conduct a "comprehensive review of missions, capabilities and America's role in the world" to inform that decision-making process, are likely to force the question of prioritization.[72] For the State Department, internal debates might include, for example, the relative weights of the communications efforts to counter violent extremism, and to build partner capacity, as well as its proposal, pending congressional approval, to establish a Bureau (instead of the current Office) for Counter-Terrorism.

Possible Implications for the Homeland[73]

It is unknown how OBL's death will affect AQ-inspired homegrown jihadist terrorists targeting the United States. On May 2, 2011, the Federal Bureau of Investigation (FBI, the Bureau) and Department of Homeland Security (DHS) issued a joint bulletin indicating that OBL's death may motivate revenge or publicity seeking homegrown jihadists to attack the United States.[74] However, it is unlikely that his death will significantly change the counterterrorism investigative efforts of the FBI, the lead agency for investigating the federal crime of terrorism.[75] Regardless, OBL's demise underscores a number of issues the Bureau confronts.

Homegrown Jihadists

It is too early to chart the specific effects of OBL's death on homegrown jihadists[76] who have accounted for more than 40 terrorist plots—4 of which resulted in attacks—since 9/11.[77] These plots and attacks reflect a global shift in terrorism toward decentralized, autonomously radicalized, violent jihadist individuals or groups who strike in their home countries.[78] Global counterterrorism efforts have made it harder for international terrorist networks to formulate plots, place their recruits in targeted countries, and carry out violent strikes in locations far from their bases of operation.[79] AQ and affiliated groups are moving "away from what we are used to, which are complex, ambitious, multilayered plots."[80]

Possible Questions

Regarding the nature of homegrown jihadist terrorism, at least four issues may emerge from OBL's death:

- Will homegrown jihadist plotting increase?
- How will his death affect the radicalization of people interested in violent jihad who live in the United States?
- How will it shape the popularity of surviving key jihadist intermediaries who inspire U.S. residents to radicalize and turn to jihadist terrorism? Intermediaries such as Anwar al-Aulaqi have allegedly influenced people involved in a number of recent homegrown terrorist plots.[81]
- Finally, because OBL's death potentially affects the radicalization process, it may be of value to assess the Administration's progress toward developing and implementing a domestic counter-radicalization strategy. It has not been entirely settled which agencies have what responsibilities when it comes to identifying domestic radicalization and interdicting attempts at terrorist recruitment.

FBI Investigations

Since 9/11, the Bureau has arguably taken a much more proactive posture, particularly regarding counterterrorism.[82] It now views its role as both "predicting and preventing" the threats facing the nation, drawing upon enhanced resources.[83] In light of this transformed role, OBL's death may offer Congress the opportunity to explore issues related to the Bureau.

- How, if at all, will the lack of so prominent a one most wanted terrorist figure alter the Bureau's mission, priorities, and allocation of resources?

- Does the FBI, and the homeland security community more broadly, have the *proactive* capacity to quickly and efficiently task its human sources (informants) to ascertain what impact OBL's death may have on homegrown jihadist extremists? This addresses a broader issue: does a coherent domestic intelligence collection strategy exist to coordinate the efforts of the FBI, the Department of Homeland Security (DHS), other federal partners, *and state and local law enforcement elements*?
- How will the FBI use strategic, big-picture intelligence to develop a corporate understanding of the ways that the domestic threat will evolve in the wake of OBL's demise? In other words, has the Bureau developed effective *predictive* capacity that can continually re-assess the changing terrorist landscape? Will the FBI alter its operations based on predictive strategic assessments in this area?

Possible Implications for U.S. Security Interests[84]

Near Term Implications for U.S. Security Interests

Some government leaders and security analysts predict that the death of OBL may be accompanied by near term threats to U.S. global security interests. Numerous reasons are offered in support of this assessment, including the need for the core, affiliates, and adherents to prove viability and relevance in response to OBL's death; retribution to avenge his killing; and the need to quickly conduct an attack due to concerns that information gleaned during the raid of OBL's compound may jeopardize operational security.

Long Term Implications for U.S. Security Interests

If it is determined that OBL remained an active decision-maker in the development of core AQ strategy and terrorist operations, his death may have negative implications for the organization's ability to continue as a viable threat to U.S. interests. While some analysts suggest that OBL may have provided some level of support to AQ affiliated organizations, most of these entities appear to be self-sufficient and it is likely regionally focused terrorism related activities would not be affected. Some fear that the death of OBL could lead to a further degradation of the standing of core AQ which in turn may lead to an attempt by a leader of an affiliated AQ organization to pursue a more aggressive global terrorist agenda in hopes of rising to place of prominence.

Implications for U.S. Foreign Policy in the Middle East

While some experts argue that OBL's limited ideological appeal and operational role in AQ suggest that the implications of his death will also be limited, senior U.S. counterterrorism officials view the death of OBL as the possible beginning of the end of AQ. In a press briefing at the White House on May 2, 2011 an unnamed senior administration official offered the following assessment of the significance of OBL's death and the prospect of continued threats to the nation.

> Without a doubt, the United States will continue to face terrorist threats. There's also no doubt that the death of Osama bin Laden marks the single greatest victory in the U.S.-led campaign to disrupt, dismantle, and defeat Al Qaeda. It is a major and essential step in bringing about Al Qaeda's eventual destruction. Although Al Qaeda may not fragment immediately, the loss of Osama bin Laden puts the group on a path of decline that will be difficult to reverse.[85]

As intelligence operations in the wake of the recent raid on OBL's compound shed light on core AQ and its affiliate's activities, policymakers may be presented with new information to help in determining how the U.S. and international counterterrorism communities might initiate changes to transnational security and foreign policy strategies. These actions coupled with the ongoing activities by individuals in the Middle East pursuing changes to the policies of current regimes may offer an opportunity for a reevaluation of U.S. foreign policy in the region. Some analysts argue that recent anti-authoritarian demonstrations and political change in some Arab states run counter to OBL's vision for the region. Others suggest that the outcome of political upheaval in the region has yet to be determined and that groups and individuals supportive of OBL's ideology may yet successfully exploit recent developments.

On May 2, Secretary of State Clinton argued that "history will record that bin Laden's death came at a time of great movements toward freedom and democracy, at a time when the people across the Middle East and North Africa are rejecting the extremist narratives and charting a path of peaceful progress based on universal rights and aspirations. There is no better rebuke to al-Qaida and its heinous ideology."[86] If demonstrators seeking change are successful in managing political transitions and ensuring lasting security in their countries, their efforts could further contribute to the decline of AQ and its ideology.

End Notes

[1] Prepared by Richard Best, Specialist in National Defense.
[2] 50 USC 413b(c)(2).
[3] 50 USC 413b(a).
[4] 50 USC 413b(e).
[5] Prepared by Michael John Garcia, Legislative Attorney.
[6] *See* Hamdi v. Rumsfeld, 542 U.S. 507, 518 (2004) (O'Connor, J., plurality opinion); *id.* at 588-589 (Thomas, J., dissenting).
[7] This report does not address potential issues under international law that may be relevant to the military operation against bin Laden. These issues include, *inter alia*, the degree to which the operation was governed by and consistent with the law of armed conflict, human rights law, customary international law concerning the right of a nation to act in self-defense to deter an impending attack, and the rights and duties of sovereign nations. Some of these issues may turn on particular facts that have not been fully brought to light at the time of this report, including whether Pakistan gave prior (or retroactive) consent to the United States to take action against bin Laden within its territory. In an op-ed published in the *Washington Post* soon after the operation, Pakistani President Asif Ali Zardari stated that:

[a]lthough the events...were not a joint operation, a decade of cooperation and partnership between the United States and Pakistan led up to the elimination of Osama bin Laden as a continuing threat to the civilized world. And we in Pakistan take some satisfaction that our early assistance in identifying an al-Qaeda courier ultimately led to this day.

Asif Ali Zardari, Op-Ed, "Pakistan Did Its Part," *Washington Post*, May 2, 2011.
[8] Although U.S. employees, by way of executive order, are generally barred from engaging in "political assassinations" abroad, U.S. policymakers have historically interpreted this prohibition as not applying to the targeting of an enemy's command and control structure during periods of armed conflict. *See generally* CRS Report RL31133, *Declarations of War and Authorizations for the Use of Military Force: Historical Background and Legal Implications*, by Jennifer K. Elsea and Richard F. Grimmett, at 35-36. *See also* Jeffrey Toobin, "Killing Osama: Was It Legal?," *New Yorker*, May 2, 2011, at http://www.newyorker.com/online/blogs/newsdesk/2011/05/killing-osama-was-it-legal.html (discussing position of George W. Bush and Obama Administrations that the prohibition on political assassinations did not apply to bin Laden or other belligerents in the conflict with AQ).
[9] The power to terminate the military conflict with Al Qaeda appears to reside exclusively with the political branches of government. The Supreme Court has recognized that the termination of a military conflict is a "political act," and it has historically refused to review the political branches' determinations of when a conflict has officially ended. Ludecke v. Watkins, 335 U.S. 160, 168-169 (1948); Baker v. Carr, 369 U.S 186, 213-214 (1962) (describing the Court's refusal to review the political branches' determination of when or whether a war has ended).
[10] Prepared by Andrew Feickert, Specialist in Military Ground Forces.
[11] Remarks by the President on Osama Bin Laden, East Room, the White House, 11:35 PM, May 1, 2011.
[12] Prepared by John Rollins, Specialist in Terrorism and National Security.
[13] Core Al Qaeda includes entities, personnel, and activities directly controlled and overseen by OBL or his designees. For additional information see CRS Report R41070, *Al Qaeda and*

Affiliates: Historical Perspective, Global Presence, and Implications for U.S. Policy, coordinated by John Rollins.

[14] Global Affiliates include organizations that have adopted some of the actions in support of the goals and beliefs of Core AQ.

[15] These entities and individuals do not have a relationship or connection with corporate AQ or an affiliated organization but are inspired by the organization's message and undertake terrorism related actions in the name of AQ.

[16] Eli Lake, "Raid provides new insight into al Qaeda operations," *Washington Times*, May 4, 2011, http://www.washingtontimes.com/news/2011/may/3/how-bin-laden-led-operations/print/#0_undefined,0_.

[17] Michael Leiter, Director, NCTC, Center for Strategic And International Studies (CSIS), December 1, 2010, The Changing Terrorist Threat and NCTC's Response, http://csis.org/files/attachments/101202_leiter_transcript.pdf.

[18] Prepared by Nicolas Cook, Specialist in African Affairs, and Christopher Blanchard, Analyst in Middle Eastern Affairs.

[19] Prepared by Alan Kronstadt, Specialist in South Asian Affairs. For broader background, see CRS Report R41307, *Pakistan: Key Current Issues and Developments*, by K. Alan Kronstadt.

[20] The location of OBL's refuge was described by a senior Obama Administration official as "relatively affluent, with lots of retired military." The structure itself, a property valued at some $1 million, was said to be roughly eight times larger than surrounding homes: "Intelligence analysts concluded that this compound was custom built to hide someone of significance." The owners of the property reportedly were ethnic Pashtun Pakistanis ("Press Briefing by Senior Administration Officials on the Killing of Osama bin Laden," May 2, 2011; "Bin Laden Hosts at Compound Were Two Pakistanis," *New York Times*, May 3, 2011).

[21] "Bin Laden's Death Likely to Deepen Suspicions of Pakistan," *New York Times*, May 2, 2011; "Failure to Discover bin Laden's Refuge Stirs Suspicion Over Pakistan's Role," *Washington Post*, May 2, 2011; "Awkward Questions Loom for Pakistan," *Financial Times* (London), May 2, 2011.

[22] "Suspicions Grow Over Whether Pakistan Aided Osama Bin laden," *Los Angeles Times*, May 2, 2011; "Press Briefing by Senior Administration Officials on the Killing of Osama bin Laden," May 2, 2011; Brennan quoted in "Osama Bin Laden Killed in U.S. Raid, Buried at Sea," *Washington Post*, May 2, 2011.

[23] Steve Coll, "Notes on the Death of Osama bin Laden," *New Yorker* (online), May 2, 2011.

[24] Daniel Markey, "More Tense Times Ahead for U.S.-Pakistan," Council on Foreign Relations First Take, May 2, 2011.

[25] A listing of some of the oftentimes categorical, high-profile Pakistani denials about OBL specifically are in "Osama bin Who?, *Foreign Policy* (online), May 2, 2011.

[26] A Foreign Ministry statement noted that AQ had "declared war on Pakistan" and said that OBL's killing "illustrates the resolve of the international community including Pakistan to fight and eliminate terrorism" and "constitutes a major setback to terrorist organizations around the world" (see the May 2, 2011, release at http://www.mofa.gov.pk/Press_Releases/2011/May/PR_150.htm).

[27] "Asif Ali Zardari, "Pakistan Did Its Part" (op-ed), *Washington Post*, May 2, 2011.

[28] See the White House's May 1, 2011, release at http://www.whitehouse.gov/the-press-office/2011/05/02/remarkspresident-osama-bin-laden.

[29] Michael O'Hanlon, "U.S.-Pakistan: Bad Union, No Divorce" (op-ed), *Politico*, May 3, 2011. See also Lisa Curtis, "The Bin Laden Aftermath: The U.S. and Pakistan Are Still Stuck With Each Other," Heritage Foundation (online), May 3, 2011.

[30] "For U.S. and Pakistan, Bin Laden Death Presents Crisis and Opportunity," CNN.com, May 2, 2011.

[31] "India Wants U.S. to Press Pakistan," *Wall Street Journal*, May 4, 2011.

[32] "Boehner: US Should Not Back Away From Pakistan," Associated Press, May 3, 2011.

[33] "Aid Attacked as Pakistan Loyalty in Doubt," *Financial Times* (London), May 3, 2011.

[34] For FY2002-FY2010, Congress appropriated about $4.43 billion in security-related assistance and $6.22 billion in economic/development/humanitarian assistance for a total of about $10.65 billion. In addition, Pakistan has received $8.88 billion in Coalition Support Fund "reimbursements" for its operational and logistical support of US-led military operations during this period.

[35] For example, at an April House hearing on South Asia, Subcommittee Chairman Representative Steve Chabot questioned Administration witnesses about why a decade of major U.S. assistance efforts had produced no obvious good results in Pakistan, commenting, "We spent all this money and they still hate us." ("House Foreign Affairs Subcommittee on Middle East and South Asia Holds Hearing on Foreign Policy Priorities in South Asia," CQ Transcriptions, April 5, 2011).

[36] Members of Congress quoted in "After Bin Laden, Pakistan May Be Greatest Casualty," Reuters, May 2, 2011. See also a May 2, 2011, statement from Senator Frank Lautenberg at http://lautenberg.senate.gov/newsroom/record.cfm?id=332658&.

[37] See, for example, a February 2011 report issued by the Inspectors General of USAID, State, and the Pentagon at http://www.usaid.gov/oig/public/special_reports/pakistan_quarterly_report_as_of_dec_31_2010.pdf.

[38] "Press Briefing by Senior Administration Officials on the Killing of Osama bin Laden," May 2, 2011.

[39] "No Proof Pakistanis Knew Bin Laden Location: U.S.," Reuters, May 3, 2011.

[40] Quoted in "Osama bin Laden Killed in U.S. Raid, Buried at Sea," *Washington Post*, May 2, 2011, and "Bin Laden Killing Was 'Joint U.S.-Pakistani Operation,'" Reuters, May 2, 2011.

[41] "Did Pakistan Know Where Bin Laden Was Hiding?," NPR (online), May 2, 2011.

[42] "Pakistan: Caught Off Guard," *Financial Times* (London), May 3, 2011.

[43] See the May 3, 2011, release at http://www.mofa.gov.pk/Press_Releases/2011/May/PR_152.htm. See also "Pakistan Defends Role, questions 'Unilateral' U.S. Action," *Washington Post*, May 3, 2011.

[44] "Pakistan, US Vow to Fight Terrorism After Bin Laden Death," Reuters, May 3, 2011.

[45] U.S. Embassy Islamabad, "Special Pakistan Media Analysis: Death of Bin Laden II" (electronic document), May 2, 2011; "Pakistan Media Analysis" (electronic document), May 3, 2011.

[46] "Bin Laden Mourned by Many in Pakistan," *Financial Times* (London), May 2, 2011; "Hundreds Join Quetta Rally to Honor Bin Laden," *Express Tribune* (Karachi), May 2, 2011; "Islamist Militants Hold Prayers for Bin Laden in Pakistan," Reuters, May 3, 2011.

[47] "Sense of Vindication and Apprehension in New Delhi," *Hindu* (Chennai), May 2, 2011; Ministry's May 2, 2011, release at http://meaindia.nic.in/mystart.php?id=530117586.

[48] "India Says Bin Laden Death Raises 'Grave Concern' Over Pakistan," Reuters, May 2, 2011; "Bin Laden Location Complicates Indian Leaders' Approach," *New York Times*, May 3, 2011.

[49] "Siddharth Varadarajan, "A Fork in the Road for the U.S. in South Asia" (op-ed), *Hindu* (Chennai), May 2, 2011.
[50] "Osama's Death Prompts India's Call for Mumbai Attack Perpetrators," *Express Tribune* (Karachi), May 2, 2011.
[51] "Afghan Officials Say Pakistan Should Have Known Bin Laden Was There," Reuters, May 4, 2011.
[52] Quoted in "Pressure Rises On U.S. To Trim Troop Numbers In Afghanistan," *Wall Street Journal*, May 3, 2011; "Osama Bin Laden: Dead, But How Did He Hide for So Long?," *Guardian* (London), May 3, 2011.
[53] "Amid Skepticism, Pakistan Calculates Its Response," *New York Times*, May 2, 2011.
[54] "Osama Bin Laden Killed Near Pakistan's West Point; Was He Really Hidden?," *Christian Science Monitor*, May 2, 2011.
[55] "Reaction Focuses on Pakistan and Saudi Arabia," *Financial Times* (London), May 2, 2011.
[56] See, for example, "The Fall of Osama" (editorial), *News International* (Rawalpindi), May 3, 2011.
[57] TTP quoted in "Pakistan Taliban Threatens Attacks After Bin Laden's Killing," Reuters, May 2, 2011; "Pakistan Fears Sharp rise in Terrorism," *Express Tribune* (Karachi), May 3, 2011.
[58] Prepared by Kenneth Katzman, Specialist in Middle Eastern Affairs.
[59] http://www.defense.gov/news/1230_1231Report.pdf
[60] Text of the Panetta interview with ABC News is at http://abcnews.go.com/print?id=11025299.
[61] Dreazen, Yochi. "Al Qaida Returning to Afghanistan for New Attacks." Nationaljournal.com. October 18, 2010.
[62] Testimony of General David Petraeus before the Senate and House Armed Services Committees, March 2011; and, Deb Riechmann. "Petraeus: Al-Qaida Is Not On Rise in Afghanistan." Associated Press, April 10, 2011.
[63] Rajiv Chandrasekaran. "U.S. sees Chance to Accelerate Negotiations With Taliban." *Washington Post*, May 4, 2011.
[64] Prepared by Catherine Dale, Specialist in International Security.
[65] President Barack Obama, *National Security Strategy*, May 2010.
[66] Department of Defense, *Quadrennial Defense Review*, February 2010.
[67] State Department, Leading through Civilian Power: The First Quadrennial Diplomacy and Development Review, 2010.
[68] See The White House, Presidential Policy Directive-1, "Organization of the National Security Council System," February 13, 2009.
[69] See President Barack Obama, Remarks by the President on Osama bin Laden, May 1, 2011, available at http://www.whitehouse.gov/blog.
[70] Ibid.
[71] See for example Lieutenant General David W. Barno, USA (ret), "A New Kind of Defense," The New York Times, May 2, 2011.
[72] See Department of Defense News Transcript, "DoD News Briefing with Secretary Gates and General Cartwright from the Pentagon," April 21, 2011, available at http://www.defense.gov/transcripts/transcript.aspx?transcriptid=4815; and "Obama Wants Defense Review, $400 Billion in Cuts," Voice of America, April 13, 2011.
[73] Prepared by Jerome Bjelopera, Specialist in Organized Crime and Terrorism.
[74] Anthony Kimery, "DHS, FBI Issue Alert on Homeland Security 'Implications' of Bin Laden's Death," Homeland Security Today, http://www.hstoday.us/blogs/the-kimery-report/blog/dhs-fbi-issue-alert-on-homeland-securityimplications-of-bin-ladens-dea/db30b2d05281d6f957159b4fbab3f3a4.html.

[75] For more on the FBI's counterterrorism investigations, see CRS Report R41780, *The Federal Bureau of Investigation and Terrorism Investigations,* by Jerome P. Bjelopera and Mark A. Randol. Pursuant to 28 Code of Federal Regulations (CFR) 0.85(l), the Attorney General has assigned responsibility to the Director of the FBI to: "(l) Exercise Lead Agency responsibility in investigating all crimes for which it has primary or concurrent jurisdiction and which involve terrorist activities or acts in preparation of terrorist activities within the statutory jurisdiction of the United States. Within the United States, this would include the collection, coordination, analysis, management and dissemination of intelligence and criminal information as appropriate." If another federal agency identifies an individual who is engaged in terrorist activities or in acts in preparation of terrorist activities, the other agency is required to promptly notify the FBI. The federal crime of terrorism is defined under law as "an offense that is calculated to influence or affect the conduct of government by intimidation or coercion, or to retaliate against government conduct 18 U.S.C. 2332b(g)(5)(A). Subparagraph B enumerates the specific crimes covered by this definition. This includes terrorist acts committed within and outside U.S. national boundaries. The extraterritorial jurisdiction for terrorism crimes is specified in 18 U.S.C. 2332b(e) and (f).

[76] For the purposes of this section, the terms "homegrown" and "domestic" describe terrorist activity or plots perpetrated within the United States or abroad by American citizens, permanent legal residents, or visitors radicalized largely within the United States. The term "jihadist" describes radicalized individuals using Islam as an ideological and/or religious justification to use violence to achieve their political goals. For more on *jihad* and AQ's global network, see CRS Report R41070, *Al Qaeda and Affiliates: Historical Perspective, Global Presence, and Implications for U.S. Policy,* coordinated by John Rollins.

[77] See CRS Report R41416, *American Jihadist Terrorism: Combating a Complex Threat,* by Jerome P. Bjelopera and Mark A. Randol. Hereafter: Bjelopera and Randol, CRS Report R41416.

[78] Marc Sageman, *Leaderless Jihad: Terror Networks in the Twenty-First Century* (Philadelphia: University of Pennsylvania Press, 2008), pp. 71, 133-146. Hereafter: Sageman, *Leaderless Jihad.*

[79] Philip Mudd, "Evaluating the Al-Qa'ida Threat to the U.S. Homeland," *CTC Sentinel,* vol. 3, no. 8 (Aug. 2010) p. 2, http://www.ctc.usma.edu/sentinel/CTCSentinel-Vol3Iss8.pdf; Dennis C. Blair, *Senate Select Committee on Intelligence: U.S. Intelligence Community Annual Threat Assessment: Statement for the Record,* Office of the Director of National Intelligence, Feb. 2, 2010, pp. 7-8, http://www.dni.gov/testimonies/20100202_testimony.pdf. Hereafter: Blair, Annual Threat Assessment, Feb. 2, 2010.

[80] Greg Miller, "Al-Qaeda's New Tactic is to Seize Shortcuts," *Los Angeles Times,* Mar. 19, 2010, http://www.latimes.com/news/nationworld/world/la-fg-qaeda19-2010 mar19,0, 1676434.story.

[81] See Bjelopera and Randol, CRS Report R41416.

[82] The FBI describes the post-9/11 changes in its approach in all major program areas at "The Intel-Driven FBI: New Approaches," http://www.fbi.gov/about-us/intelligence/intel-driven/new-approaches.

[83] U.S. Congress, House Committee on Appropriations, Subcommittee on Commerce, Justice, Science, and Related Agencies, *Statement of Robert S. Mueller, III; Director FBI,* Federal Bureau of Investigations FY2012 Budget Hearing, 112th Cong., 1st sess., April 6, 2011, http://www.fbi.gov/news/testimony/fbi-budget-for-fiscal-year-2012.

[84] Prepared by John Rollins, Specialist in Terrorism and National Security, 7-5529.

[85] The White House. May 2, 2011, Press Briefing by Senior Administration Officials on the Killing of Osama bin Laden.

[86] State Department, *Remarks on the Killing of Usama bin Ladin*, Remarks by Secretary Clinton, May 2, 2011, http://www.state.gov/secretary/rm/2011/05/162339.htm.

In: The Death of Osama bin Laden ...
Editor: Raymond V. Donahue

ISBN: 978-1-61470-479-9
© 2011 Nova Science Publishers, Inc.

Chapter 2

AL QAEDA AND AFFILIATES: HISTORICAL PERSPECTIVE, GLOBAL PRESENCE, AND IMPLICATIONS FOR U.S. POLICY[*]

John Rollins

SUMMARY

Al Qaeda (AQ) has evolved into a significantly different terrorist organization than the one that perpetrated the September 11, 2001, attacks. At the time, Al Qaeda was composed mostly of a core cadre of veterans of the Afghan insurgency against the Soviet Union, with a centralized leadership structure made up mostly of Egyptians. Most of the organization's plots either emanated from the top or were approved by the leadership. Some analysts describe pre-9/11 Al Qaeda as akin to a corporation, with Osama Bin Laden acting as an agile Chief Executive Officer issuing orders and soliciting ideas from subordinates.

Some would argue that the Al Qaeda of that period no longer exists. Out of necessity, due to pressures from the security community, in the ensuing years it has transformed into a diffuse global network and philosophical movement composed of dispersed nodes with varying degrees of independence. Al Qaeda franchises or affiliated groups active in countries such as Yemen and Somalia now represent critical power centers in the larger movement. Some affiliates receive money, training,

---

[*] This is an edited, reformatted and augmented version of a Congressional Research Service publication, CRS Report for Congress R41070, from www.crs.gov, dated January 25, 2011.

and weapons; others look to the core leadership in Pakistan for strategic guidance, theological justification, and a larger narrative of global struggle. Over the past year senior government officials have assessed the trajectory of Al Qaeda to be "less centralized command and control, (with) no clear center of gravity, and likely rising and falling centers of gravity, depending on where the U.S. and the international focus is for that period." While a degraded corporate Al Qaeda may be welcome news to many, a trend has emerged over the past few years that some view as more difficult to detect, if not potentially more lethal.

The Al Qaeda network today also comprises semi-autonomous or self radicalized actors, who often have only peripheral or ephemeral ties to either the core cadre in Pakistan or affiliated groups elsewhere. According to U.S. officials Al Qaeda cells and associates are located in over 70 countries. Sometimes these individuals never leave their home country but are radicalized with the assistance of others who have traveled abroad for training and indoctrination through the use of modern technologies. The name "Qaeda" means "base" or "foundation," upon which its members hope to build a robust, geographically diverse network.

Understanding the origins of Al Qaeda, its goals, current activities, and prospective future pursuits is key to developing sound U.S. strategies, policies, and programs. Appreciating the adaptive nature of Al Qaeda as a movement and the ongoing threat it projects onto U.S. global security interests assists in many facets of the national security enterprise, including securing the homeland; congressional legislative process and oversight; alignment of executive branch resources and coordination efforts; and prioritization of foreign assistance.

The focus of this report is on the history of Al Qaeda, known (or attributed) actions and suspected capabilities of the organization and non-aligned entities, and an analysis of select regional Al Qaeda affiliates. This report may be updated as events warrant.

BACKGROUND[1]

The Al Qaeda movement has transformed in recent years: some of the strategic objectives of the original, or core, organization have remained consistent while the views and goals of new affiliates, leaders, and recruits have evolved and become more diverse. Osama Bin Laden's Al Qaeda and the affiliated organizations that ascribe their actions to his violence-based philosophy continue to desire to attack the United States and its global interests. In a June 2010 speech, the Principal Deputy Coordinator for Counterterrorism for the Department of State stated that "while (core) Al

Qaeda is now struggling in some areas the threat it poses is becoming more widely distributed, more geographically diverse. The rise of affiliated groups such as Al Qaeda the Arabian Peninsula and Al Qaeda in the Islamic Maghreb is a new and important development and is also a troubling development."[2] In addressing threats to global security interests before the Senate Homeland Security and Governmental Affairs Committee in September 2010, the U.S. intelligence community assessed that "the range of Al Qaeda's core, affiliated, allied, and inspired U.S. citizens and residents plotting against the homeland during the past year suggests the threat against the West has become more complex and underscores the challenges of identifying and countering a more diverse array of homeland plotting."[3]

Due in large part to the actions of the U.S. government, core Al Qaeda, reportedly located in Pakistan, is under tremendous pressure. U.S. and coalition force's military and intelligence operations appear to have degraded the core's capacity for conducting large catastrophic operations similar to the attacks of September 11, 2001. The core organization's apparent inability to commit large-scale attacks in recent years has led some analysts to question the relevancy, capabilities, and competency of the group.[4] However, during the 2010 Annual Threat Assessment hearing in front of the Senate Select Committee on Intelligence, Dennis C. Blair, Director of National Intelligence (DNI), observed that while "important progress has been made against the threat to the U.S. homeland over the past few years, I cannot reassure you that the danger is gone. We face a persistent terrorist threat from Al Qaeda and potentially others who share its anti-Western ideology. A major terrorist attack may emanate from either outside or inside the United States."[5] In addressing how the U.S. might assess whether the organization remains a viable entity the DNI further stated, "until counterterrorism pressure on Al Qaeda's place of refuge, key lieutenants, and operative cadre outpaces the group's ability to recover, Al Qaeda will retain its capability to mount an attack."[6]

While pressure from the international community on core Al Qaeda appears to have limited the group's ability to undertake a catastrophic terrorist attack on U.S. interests, many terrorist groups and cells located throughout the world are affiliating their actions with the organization. Al Qaeda continues to attract potential recruits and possess an ability to influence and support global organizations with similar goals and philosophical objectives. The often-termed jihadi movement[7] has increasingly become an issue of concern for senior members of the U.S. national security community. During the 2010 Annual Threat Assessment hearing DNI Blair noted the following:

Al Qaeda will continue its efforts to encourage key regional affiliates and jihadist networks to pursue a global agenda. A few Al Qaeda regional affiliates and jihadist networks have exhibited an intent or capability to attack inside the homeland. Some regional nodes and allies have grown in strength and independence over the last two years and have begun to project operationally outside their regions.[8]

Though Al Qaeda affiliated entities have attempted numerous deadly terrorist attacks in recent years,[9] some analysts view these operations as evidence of desperation signifying that the core organization and its affiliates are no longer capable of launching a large-scale catastrophic terrorist attack directed at U.S. interests. These analysts suggest that recent attempted acts are an acknowledgment that the destructive capabilities of corporate Al Qaeda and those individuals with similar philosophical goals are actually on the decline and are indicative of an organization desperate to prove its continued viability. Others, however, suggest that this recent trend may be indicative of an organization becoming more selective and sophisticated in the operations it pursues and adopting a model of encouraging affiliates and sympathizers to undertake smaller-scale acts to divert international attention and resources away from planning and preparations for larger, more catastrophic, attacks.

Recognition of a more resilient enemy may have been enunciated in a September 22, 2010, statement by the Director of the Federal Bureau of Investigation (FBI) before the Senate Committee on Homeland Security and Governmental Affairs:

> the level of cooperation among Al Qaeda and other terrorist groups has changed in the past year suggesting that this collaboration and resulting threat to the homeland will increase. By sharing financial resources, training, tactical and operations expertise, and recruits, these groups have been able to withstand significant counterterrorism pressure from the United States, coalition, and local government forces.[10]

Similarly, in acknowledging the government's challenge of transitioning from an almost exclusive focus on core Al Qaeda to also attempting to assess the capabilities of numerous smaller groups that are more opaque, the Secretary of Homeland Security stated "the terrorist threat changes quickly and we have observed important changes in the threat even since this Committee convened a similar hearing last year. The threat is evolving in several ways that make it more difficult for law enforcement or the intelligence community to detect and disrupt plots."[11]

Notwithstanding the challenges associated with continuing to limit core Al Qaeda's planning and destructive capabilities while also attempting to thwart potential attacks by lesser-known affiliated entities, some in the counterterrorism community suggest that the organization and the philosophical following it has spawned are significantly degraded. A December 2010 report issued by West Point's Combating Terrorism Center noted the following:

> More than twenty years after its creation, Al Qaeda shows clear signs of decline. The group has lost many of its key operational leaders to arrest or assassination; a number of Al Qaeda franchises—including in Saudi Arabia, Iraq and Algeria—have been substantially weakened or defeated; and a host of ideological challenges, including recantations from prominent jihadis themselves, have compelled Al Qaeda to spend valuable time defending its reputation and actions. These setbacks and others suggest that Al Qaeda is not any closer to achieving its long-term goals than it was on 10 September 2001.[12]

Likewise, others in the national security community have offered observations that help explain why Al Qaeda may be an organization on the decline and possibly in jeopardy of losing its appeal to potential followers. According to the non-governmental Bipartisan Policy Center four key strategic issues are contributing to the demise of Al Qaeda: indiscriminate killing of Muslims, the lack of a political movement to represent the organization's interests, an ever-growing list of enemies, and the lack of a desirable vision that sustains interest in the group and its ideology (see "Al Qaeda's Global Strategy and Implications for U.S. Policy" below).[13]

Given recent discussions regarding the potential demise of Al Qaeda, some counterterrorism observers suggest that such assessments may be premature. In an article published in the December 2010 edition of Studies in Conflict and Terrorism, the authors argue that the organization's infrastructure and ideology are resilient and have the ability to endure external pressures from the international security community. The authors find that "although in recent years Al Qaeda has adopted more ideological and inspirational characteristics, it still exists as a group, and possesses, first and foremost, operational characteristics of guerilla and terrorist organization."[14]

Jihad, Al Qaeda, and other Violent Islamist Groups

The Arabic word *jihad* is derived from a verb that means "to struggle, strive, or exert oneself." It appears in the Quran in the context of calls to strive for the advancement of Islam and to make a personal commitment to struggle "in the cause of God." At its most general level, *jihad* denotes taking action on behalf of Islam and fellow Muslims, and thereby improving one's standing as a pious member of the religious community. The concept has been understood by Muslims in various ways over time to include fighting (*qital*) against those who oppose the advancement of Islam or who harm Muslims, fundraising for Islamic causes, proselytizing, doing charitable work, and struggling against personal desires. Historically, key Sunni and Shi'a religious texts such as collections of sayings and deeds of the prophet Mohammed (*hadith*) most often referred to *jihad* in terms of religiously-approved fighting on behalf of Islam and Muslims. Some Muslims have emphasized nonviolent social and personal means of *jihad* or have sought to shape the modern meaning of the term to refer to fighting only under defensive circumstances.

The term Islamist refers to groups and individuals who support a formal political role for Islam through the implementation of Islamic law (*sharia*) by the state, political action through a religious party, or the creation of a religious system of governance. Islamists differ in their theological views and political priorities. Islamists may use nonviolent or violent tactics in pursuit of local, national, or transnational agendas.

The early years of the Islamic faith in 7th century Arabia were marked by conflict between Muslims and non-Muslims and among Muslims themselves. The positive connotations early Muslims attached to *jihad* on behalf of their new community makes the concept an attractive ideological tool for contemporary violent Sunni Islamist groups. In attempting to mobilize Muslims for collective action, many of these groups seek to cloak themselves in legitimacy by associating themselves with Mohammed and the first three generations of Muslims (*al salaf al saalih*).

Most Al Qaeda-produced ideological material reflects the group's shared view of *jihad* as, first and foremost, an individual duty to fight on behalf of Islam and Muslims, and, in some cases, to offensively attack Muslims or non-Muslims who are deemed insufficiently pious or who oppose enforcement of Islamic principles and religious law.

Al Qaeda and other violent Islamist groups seek to convince fellow Muslims that the use of violence as a tactic and support for violent groups is religiously justified and required. To do so, they draw on the Quran and other Islamic religious texts and adapt historical events—especially the experiences of Mohammed and the early Islamic community—to current circumstances.

Al Qaeda's uncompromising approach to the practice of Islam, its use of violence against Muslims, and its views about the illegitimacy of democracy often put them at odds with other Muslims. Some conservative Sunni Muslim clerics also reject some violent Islamist interpretations of Islamic principles, including *jihad*. Since the 1980s, groups advocating violent *jihad* have differed over the relative importance of targeting local governments and societies or targeting the United States and other entities believed to be hostile to Muslims or supportive of hostile local governments. Al Qaeda's transnational appeals to Muslims in Europe and North America often blend rhetoric about foreign conflicts and occupation with calls to join insurgencies or carry out terrorist attacks.

Overall, *jihad* remains a contested concept among Muslims and non-Muslims alike. Some observers resist referring to the actions of Al Qaeda and other violent groups in terms of *jihad* because they believe that such usage unfairly links violence to an important concept in Islam and implies that violent groups are acting on behalf of Islam in a legitimate or praiseworthy manner. Others believe that references to *jihad* and jihadists in discussions of political violence and Islam are justified because Muslims historically have linked *jihad* to conflict and, at present, some violent individuals or groups that claim to be acting on behalf of Islam or Muslims self-identify as *jihadis* or *mujahidin*. As such, these observers argue that directly addressing differing views on *jihad* is critical for counteracting the messages and agendas of violent Islamist groups.

This report uses the term "jihad" to denote violent Sunni Islamists' understanding of the concept as a religious call to arms and uses the terms "jihadi" and "jihadist" to refer to groups and individuals whose statements indicate that they share such an understanding of jihad and who advocate or use violence against the United States or in support of transnational Islamist agendas. Alternative terms include "violent Islamist" or "militant Islamist."

For further discussion of *jihad* in the context of Al Qaeda and other violent Islamist organizations, see Thomas Hegghammer, "Jihadi-Salafis or Revolutionaries? On Religion and Politics in the Study of Militant

> Islamism," in Roel Meijer, ed., *Global Salafism*, Hurst/Columbia University Press, New York, 2009, pp. 244-266; Steven Brooke, "Jihadist Strategic Debates before 9/11," *Studies in Conflict & Terrorism*, 31, 2008, pp. 201–226; and, Assaf Moghadam and Brian Fishman (eds.), *Self-Inflicted Wounds: Debates and Divisions within al-Qa'ida and its Periphery*, United States Military Academy Combating Terrorism Center, December 2010. For background on the concept of *jihad* in Islam, see Rudolph Peters, *Jihad in Classical and Modern Islam*, Markus Weiner Publishers, 2008; David Cook, *Understanding Jihad*, University of California Press, 2005; Michael Bonner, *Jihad in Islamic History*, Princeton University Press, 2006; and Reuven Firestone, *Jihad*, Oxford University Press, 1999.

ORIGINS OF AL QAEDA[15]

The primary founder of Al Qaeda, Osama Bin Laden, was born in July 1957, the 17th of 20 sons of a Saudi construction magnate of Yemeni origin. Most Saudis are conservative Sunni Muslims, and Bin Laden, conservative from a young age, appears to have adopted militant Islamist views while studying at King Abdul Aziz University in Jeddah, Saudi Arabia. There he attended lectures by Muhammad Qutb, brother of Sayyid Qutb, the key ideologue of a major Sunni Islamist movement, the Muslim Brotherhood.[16] Another of Bin Laden's inspirations was Abdullah al Azzam, a major figure in the Jordanian branch of the Muslim Brotherhood. Azzam is identified by some experts as the intellectual architect of the *jihad* against the 1979-1989 Soviet occupation of Afghanistan, and ultimately of Al Qaeda itself; he cast the Soviet invasion as an attempted conquest by a non-Muslim power of sacred Muslim territory and people.[17]

Bin Laden made his first visit to Afghanistan a few years after the December 1979 Soviet invasion, and then relocated to areas of Pakistan near the border with Afghanistan by 1986. He reportedly used some of his personal funds to establish himself as a donor to the Afghan *mujahedin* and a recruiter of Arab and other Islamic volunteers for the war.[18] In 1984, Azzam and bin Laden structured this assistance by establishing a network of recruiting and fund-raising offices in the Arab world, Europe, and the United States. That network was called the *Maktab al Khidamat* (Services Office), also known as *Al Khifah*; many experts consider the *Maktab* to be the organizational forerunner of Al Qaeda. Another major figure who utilized the *Maktab* network to recruit for the anti-Soviet *jihad* was Umar Abd al Rahman (also known as "the blind shaykh"), the spiritual leader of radical Egyptian Islamist group Al Jihad. Bin Laden apparently also made occasional forays across the border into Afghanistan during the anti-Soviet war; he reportedly participated in a 1986 battle in Jalalabad and an April 1987 frontal assault by foreign volunteers against Afghan forces equipped with Soviet armor. According to some experts, Bin Laden has said he was exposed to a Soviet chemical attack and slightly injured in the latter battle.[19]

During this period, most U.S. officials perceived the volunteers as positive contributors to the effort to expel Soviet forces from Afghanistan, and U.S. officials made no apparent effort to stop the recruitment of the non-Afghan volunteers for the war. U.S. officials have repeatedly denied that the United States directly supported the non-Afghan volunteers.[20] The United States did covertly finance (about $3 billion during 1981-1991) and arm (via Pakistan) the Afghan *mujahedin* factions, particularly the Islamic fundamentalist Afghan factions, fighting Soviet forces. By almost all accounts, it was the Afghan *mujahedin* factions, not the Arab volunteer fighters, that were decisive in persuading the Soviet Union to pull out of Afghanistan. During this period, Bin Laden, Azzam, and Abd al Rahman were not known to have openly advocated, undertaken, or planned any direct attacks against the United States, although they all were critical of U.S. support for Israel in the Middle East.

In 1988, toward the end of the Soviet occupation, Bin Laden, Azzam, and other associates began contemplating how, and to what end, the Islamist volunteer network they had organized could be utilized. U.S. intelligence estimates of the size of that network were between 10,000 and 20,000; however, not all of these necessarily supported or participated in Al Qaeda terrorist activities.[21]

Azzam apparently wanted this "Al Qaeda" (Arabic for "the base") organization—as they began terming the organization in 1988—to become an Islamic "rapid reaction force," available to intervene wherever Muslims were perceived to be threatened. Bin Laden differed with Azzam, hoping instead to dispatch the Al Qaeda activists to their home countries to try to topple secular, pro-Western Arab leaders, such as President Hosni Mubarak of Egypt and Saudi Arabia's royal family.

Some attribute the Bin Laden-Azzam differences to the growing influence on Bin Laden of the Egyptians in his inner circle, such as Abd al Rahman, who wanted to use Al Qaeda's resources to install an Islamic state in Egypt. Another close Egyptian confidant was Ayman al-Zawahiri, operational leader of Al Jihad in Egypt. Like Abd al Rahman, Zawahiri had been imprisoned but ultimately acquitted for the October 1981 assassination of Egyptian President Anwar Sadat, and he permanently left Egypt in 1985 and arrived in the Afghanistan theater in 1986 after an intervening period in Saudi Arabia. In the Afghanistan conflict, he used his medical training to tend to fighters wounded in the war. In November 1989, Azzam was assassinated, and some allege that Bin Laden might have been responsible for the killing to resolve this power struggle. Following Azzam's death, Bin Laden gained control of the *Maktab*'s funds and organizational mechanisms. Abd al Rahman came to the United States in 1990 from Sudan and was convicted in October 1995 for terrorist plots related to the February 1993 bombing of the World Trade Center in New York.

The Threat Unfolds

The August 2, 1990, Iraqi invasion of Kuwait apparently reinforced Bin Laden's turn from a de-facto U.S. ally against the Soviet Union into one of its most active adversaries. Bin Laden had returned home to Saudi Arabia in 1989, after the completion of the Soviet withdrawal from Afghanistan that February. While back home, he lobbied Saudi officials not to host U.S. combat troops to defend Saudi Arabia against an Iraqi invasion, arguing instead for the raising of a *"mujahedin"* army to oust Iraq from Kuwait. His idea was rebuffed by the Saudi leadership as impractical, causing Bin Laden's falling out with the royal family, and 500,000 U.S. troops deployed to Saudi Arabia to oust Iraqi forces from Kuwait in "Operation Desert Storm" (January 16-February 28, 1991). About 6,000 U.S. forces, mainly Air Force, remained in the kingdom during 1991-2003 to conduct operations to contain Iraq. Although the post-1991 U.S. force in Saudi Arabia was relatively small and confined to Saudi military facilities, bin Laden and his followers painted the U.S. forces as occupiers of sacred Islamic ground and the Saudi royal family as facilitator of that "occupation."

In 1991, after his rift with the Saudi leadership, Bin Laden relocated to Sudan, buying property there which he used to host and train Al Qaeda militants—this time, for use against the United States and its interests, as well as for *jihad* operations in the Balkans, Chechnya, Kashmir, and the Philippines. During the early 1990s, he also reportedly funded Saudi Islamist dissidents in London, including Saad Faqih, organized as the "Movement for Islamic Reform in Arabia (MIRA)."[22] Bin Laden himself remained in Sudan until the Sudanese government, under U.S. and Egyptian pressure, expelled him in May 1996; he then returned to Afghanistan and helped the Taliban gain and maintain control of Afghanistan. (The Taliban captured Kabul in September 1996.)

Bin Laden and Zawahiri apparently believed that the only way to bring Islamic regimes to power was to oust from the region the perceived backer of secular regional regimes, the United States. During the 1990s, bin Laden and Zawahiri transformed Al Qaeda into a global threat to U.S. national security, culminating in the September 11, 2001, attacks. By this time, Al Qaeda had become a coalition of factions of radical Islamic groups operating throughout the Muslim world, mostly groups opposing their governments. Cells and associates have been located in over 70 countries, according to U.S. officials.

The pre-September 11 roster of attacks against the United States and U.S. interests that are widely attributed to Al Qaeda included the following:

- In 1992, Al Qaeda claimed responsibility for bombing a hotel in Yemen where 100 U.S. military personnel were awaiting deployment to Somalia for Operation Restore Hope. No one was killed.
- A growing body of information about central figures in the February 1993 bombing of the World Trade Center in New York, particularly the reputed key bomb maker Ramzi Ahmad Yusuf, suggests possible Al Qaeda involvement. As noted above, Abd al Rahman was convicted for plots related to this attack.
- Al Qaeda claimed responsibility for arming Somali factions who battled U.S. forces there in October 1993, and who killed 18 U.S. special operations forces in Mogadishu in October 1993.
- In June 1995, in Ethiopia, members of Al Qaeda allegedly aided the Egyptian militant Islamic Group in a nearly successful assassination attempt against the visiting Mubarak.
- The four Saudi nationals who confessed to a November 1995 bombing of a U.S. military advisory facility in Riyadh, Saudi Arabia, claimed on Saudi television to have been inspired by bin Laden and other radical Islamist leaders. Five Americans were killed in that attack. Saudi leaders do not attribute the attacks directly to Bin Laden or Al Qaeda.
- The September 11 Commission report indicated that Al Qaeda might have had a hand in the June 1996 bombing of the Khobar Towers complex near Dhahran, Saudi Arabia. However, then-director of the FBI Louis Freeh previously attributed that attack primarily to Saudi

Shiite dissidents working with Iranian agents. Nineteen U.S. airmen were killed.
- Al Qaeda allegedly was responsible for the August 1998 bombings of U.S. embassies in Kenya and Tanzania, which killed about 300. On August 20, 1998, the United States launched a cruise missile strike against bin Laden's training camps in Afghanistan, reportedly missing him by a few hours.
- In December 1999, U.S. and Jordanian authorities separately thwarted related Al Qaeda plots against religious sites in Jordan and apparently against the Los Angeles international airport.
- In October 2000, Al Qaeda activists attacked the U.S.S. Cole in a ship-borne suicide bombing while the Cole was docked the harbor of Aden, Yemen. The ship was damaged and 17 sailors were killed.

AFGHANISTAN[23]

Background and Threat Assessment

Afghanistan was Al Qaeda's main base of operations during Osama bin Laden's residence there in 1996-2001. Al Qaeda operatives—and their protectors in the Taliban regime that ruled those same years—were captured or mostly driven out of Afghanistan during the major combat phase of Operation Enduring Freedom, which began on October 7, 2001, and continues today. As reiterated by the December 16, 2010, summary of a late 2010 Administration review on Afghanistan, the U.S. mission in Afghanistan, now carried out by 98,000 U.S. forces plus about 41,000 forces from partner countries, is to deny Al Qaeda safe haven in Afghanistan and to deny the Taliban the ability to overthrow the Afghan government.[24]

U.S. commanders say that Al Qaeda militants are more facilitators of militant incursions into Afghanistan than active fighters in the Afghan insurgency. Small numbers of Al Qaeda members—including Arabs, Uzbeks, and Chechens—have been captured or killed in battles in Afghanistan itself over the past few years, according to U.S. commanders. Some of these fighters apparently belong to Al Qaeda affiliates such as the Islamic Movement of Uzbekistan (IMU). In the most direct Administration statement on the strength of Al Qaeda in Afghanistan itself, Director of Central Intelligence Leon Panetta said on June 27, 2010, that Al Qaeda fighters in Afghanistan itself might number 50-100.[25] However, since that statement, some NATO/ISAF officials said in October 2010, however, that Al Qaeda cells may be moving back into remote areas of Kunar and Nuristan provinces.[26]

Al Qaeda's top leadership has eluded U.S. forces in Afghanistan and other efforts in Pakistan. In December 2001, in the course of the post-September 11 major combat effort, U.S. Special Operations Forces and Central Intelligence Agency operatives reportedly narrowed Osama bin Laden's location to the Tora Bora mountains in Nangarhar Province (30 miles west of the Khyber Pass crossing between Afghanistan and Pakistan), but the Afghan militia fighters who were the bulk of the fighting force did not prevent his escape. Some U.S. military and intelligence officers (such as Gary Berntsen and Dalton Fury, who have written books on the battle)[27] have questioned the U.S. decision to rely mainly on Afghan forces in this engagement, asserting that Afghan factions may have accepted funds or tribal and clan overtures to permit the escape of the Al Qaeda leaders.

Implications for U.S. Policy

Bin Laden and his close ally, Egyptian militant leader Ayman al-Zawahiri, were presumed to be on the Pakistani side of the border. After years in which U.S. and regional officials said there was virtually no information on their whereabouts, CNN quoted a NATO official on October 18, 2010 that assessments from the U.S.-led coalition now say the two were likely in a settled area near the border with Afghanistan, and not living in a very remote uninhabited area.[28] A U.S. strike reportedly missed Zawahiri by a few hours in the village of Damadola, Pakistan, in January 2006, suggesting that there has sometimes been actionable intelligence on his movements.[29] From their redoubt, these leaders continue to occasionally issue audiotapes and statements inspiring supporters and operatives to continue to be looking for ways to attack the U.S. homeland or U.S. allies and to threaten such attacks. On the ninth anniversary of the September 11, 2001 attacks on the United States, some U.S. observers said it was still significant to try to capture bin Laden if for no other reason than for symbolic value.

Among other efforts that have targeted senior Al Qaeda leadership, a strike in late January 2008, in an area near Damadola, killed Abu Laith al-Libi, a reported senior Al Qaeda figure who purportedly masterminded, among other operations, the bombing at Bagram Air Base in February 2007 when Vice President Cheney was visiting. In August 2008, an airstrike was confirmed to have killed Al Qaeda chemical weapons expert Abu Khabab al-

Masri, and two senior operatives allegedly involved in the 1998 embassy bombings in Africa reportedly were killed by a Predator strike in January 2009. Press reports in early September 2010 say that Al Qaeda's former spokesman, Kuwait-born Sulayman Abu Ghaith, may have been released from house arrest by Iran and allowed to proceed to Pakistan.

These types of strikes have become more frequent under President Obama, indicating that the Administration sees the tactic as effective in preventing attacks. Unmanned vehicle strikes are also increasingly used on the Afghanistan battlefield itself and against Al Qaeda affiliated militants in such countries as Yemen.

PAKISTAN[30]

Background and Threat Assessment

U.S. officials remain concerned that senior Al Qaeda terrorists operate on Pakistani territory, perhaps with some level of impunity, and that the group appears to have increased its influence among the myriad Islamist militant groups operating along the Pakistan-Afghanistan border, as well as in the densely populated Punjab province. Al Qaeda forces that fled Afghanistan with their Taliban supporters remain active in Pakistan and reportedly have extensive, mutually supportive links with indigenous Pakistani terrorist groups that conduct anti-Western and anti-India attacks, including the November 2008 assault on Mumbai, India, that left some 173 people dead and was perpetrated by the Pakistan-based Lashkar-e-Taiba, a group considered closely linked with Al Qaeda.[31] Al Qaeda founder Osama Bin Laden and his deputy, Egyptian Islamist radical Ayman alZawahiri, were widely believed to be hiding in northwestern Pakistan, along with most other senior operatives.[32] Al Qaeda leaders have issued statements encouraging Pakistani Muslims to "resist" the American "occupiers" in Pakistan (and Afghanistan), and to fight against Pakistan's "U.S.- allied politicians and officers."[33] Recent unclassified assessments place more than 300 Al Qaeda operatives in Pakistan's tribal areas.[34]

Al Qaeda is widely believed to maintain camps in western Pakistan where foreign extremists receive training in terrorist operations. At least 150 Westerners reportedly have attended these camps since 2008. As military pressure has mounted on Al Qaeda, these camps may have become smaller and more mobile. In 2010, the flow of aspiring Western terrorist recruits continued, and the consensus view of analysts is that Al Qaeda's sanctuary in Pakistan's Federally Administered Tribal Areas (FATA) remains a crucial threat.[35] Recent U.S. attention has focused on the threat posed by Yemen-based Al Qaeda elements who are likely to be receiving strategic and philosophical support from their Pakistan-based allies.[36]

A 2007 National Intelligence Estimate on terrorist threats to the U.S. homeland concluded that Al Qaeda "has protected or regenerated key elements of its Homeland attack capability, including a safehaven in [Pakistan's FATA], operational lieutenants, and its top leadership."[37] In early 2009, the Obama Administration declared that the "core goal" of the United States should be to "disrupt, dismantle, and defeat Al Qaeda and its safe havens in Pakistan, and to prevent their return to Pakistan or Afghanistan."[38] The President continues to assert that Al Qaeda represents the top-most threat to U.S. security, and the State Department's *Country Reports on Terrorism 2009* (released August 2010) flatly stated that "In 2009, Al Qaeda's core in Pakistan remained the most formidable terrorist organization targeting the U.S. homeland."[39]

It appears that Al Qaeda's South Asia regional strategy has in recent years shifted toward greater emphasis on combating its Pakistani enemies. As articulated by one analyst,

> Al Qaeda has utilized its media prowess and ideological authority to discredit the Pakistani state and promote cooperation among a variety of Pakistani militants to challenge the state's authority and undermine its support for U.S. efforts in Afghanistan.[40]

By justifying and rallying support for the Pakistani jihad, providing "force multiplier" facilitation of attacks inside Pakistan, and acting as a mediator and coalition-builder among Pakistan's myriad Islamist militant groups, Al Qaeda's leadership has sought to both preserve its geographic base and mitigate the negative effects of militarized U.S. and Pakistani actions against it.[41]

While taking questions from senior Pakistani journalists during a late 2009 visit to Pakistan, Secretary of State Hillary Clinton offered a pointed expression of U.S. concerns that some elements of official Pakistan maintain sympathy for most-wanted Islamist terrorists:

> Al Qaeda has had safe haven in Pakistan since 2002. I find it hard to believe that nobody in [the Pakistani] government knows where they are and couldn't get them if they really wanted to. And maybe that's the case. Maybe they're not gettable.... I don't know what the reasons are that Al

Qaeda has safe haven in your country, but let's explore it and let's try to be honest about it and figure out what we can do.[42]

Pakistani officials are resentful of such suggestions. Islamabad reportedly has remanded to U.S. custody roughly 500 Al Qaeda fugitives since 2001, including several senior alleged operatives. U.S. officials have lauded Pakistani military operations against Al Qaeda- and Taliban-allied militants in western tribal areas beginning in late 2009 and continuing at a limited pace to date; Islamabad has devoted up to 200,000 regular and paramilitary troops to this effort. They also claim that drone-launched U.S. missile attacks and Pakistan's pressing of military offensives against extremist groups in the border areas have meaningfully disrupted Al Qaeda activities there while inflicting heavy losses on their cadre.[43] The Obama Administration has significantly accelerated the pace of unmanned aerial vehicle (drone) strikes in western Pakistan, with the reported number of such strikes rising from 34 in 2008 and 53 in 2009 to more than 110 in 2010.[44] In addition, a years-long effort by Western intelligence agencies to penetrate Al Qaeda with moles and informants may be paying off, despite the fact that dozens of such infiltrators have been executed in western Pakistan since 2001.[45]

The Tehrik-e Taliban Pakistan (TTP or "Pakistani Taliban") is an umbrella organization of Islamist militant groups in western Pakistan that has more closely allied itself with Al Qaeda in recent years.[46] The August 2009 death of TTP leader Baitullah Mehsud was a notable success for U.S. strategy, as were the May 2010 death of Al Qaeda's third-ranking operative, Egyptian national Mustafa Abu al-Yazid, and that of his successor, Egyptian national Sheikh Fateh, four months later. All three deaths were assumed caused by U.S.-launched missiles. Yet a flurry of lethal suicide bomb attacks on urban Pakistani targets in late 2009 continued (at a significantly reduced pace) in 2010 and demonstrates the resiliency of regional militant groups. New Al Qaeda-allied militant leaders have arisen to pose major threats beyond the region. Among the most notable is Ilyas Kashmiri, the commander of the Pakistan-based Harakat-ul Jihad Islami (HuJI, or Movement for an Islamic Holy War), a militant group formed in the 1980s and now closely aligned with Al Qaeda.[47]

Some analysts worry that successful drone operations are driving Al Qaeda fighters into Pakistani cities where they will be harder to target, while also exacerbating already significant anti-American sentiments among the Pakistani people. Senior Al Qaeda figures have become more active in the Pakistani megacity of Karachi, about 500 miles south of the FATA; some have been captured there through joint U.S.-Pakistani intelligence operations. Al Qaeda may increasingly be focused on provoking conflict in both Karachi and in Pakistan's "cultural capital" of Lahore as a means of diverting the Pakistani Army and establishing new safe havens.[48]

Despite Al Qaeda enduring some disruptions in its operations in Pakistan, the organization has been resurgent with anti-U.S. terrorists appearing to have benefitted from what some analysts have called a Pakistani policy of appeasement in western tribal areas near the Afghan border. Some Pakistani and Western security officials have seen Islamabad losing its war against religious militancy and Al Qaeda forces enjoying new areas in which to operate, due in part to the Pakistan Army's poor counterinsurgency capabilities and to the central government's eroded legitimacy. At the same time, the Pakistan Army appears hesitant to expand its ground offensive operations into western tribal agencies to which Al Qaeda and other militant leaders are believed to have fled (North Waziristan perhaps primary among these), and which may allow Al Qaeda to continue using the rugged region as a base of operations.

Implications for U.S. Policy

In the wake of the September 2001 terrorist attacks on the United States, President Bush launched major military operations in South and Southwest Asia as part of the global U.S.-led antiterrorism effort. Operation Enduring Freedom in Afghanistan has seen substantive success with the vital assistance of neighboring Pakistan. President Obama has bolstered the U.S. military presence in Afghanistan with a central goal of neutralizing the Al Qaeda threat emanating from the region. Yet neighboring Pakistan continues to be an "epicenter of terrorism" from which threats to the United States and other western countries continue to emanate. Recently uncovered evidence suggests that the 9/11 hijackers were themselves based in western Pakistan in early 2001 and, by one account, Al Qaeda and its Pakistani affiliates provided operational direction in 38% of the serious terrorist plots against Western countries since 2004.[49] As tensions between Pakistan and India remain tense more than two years after the November 2008 terrorist attack on Mumbai, India, Secretary of Defense Robert Gates has warned that groups under Al Qaeda's Pakistan "syndicate" are actively seeking to destabilize the entire South Asia region, perhaps through a another successful major terrorist attack in India that could provoke all-out war between the region's two largest and nuclear-armed states.[50]

U.S. policy options to address the Al Qaeda threat in Pakistan are limited. While Al Qaeda remains widely unpopular among the Pakistani public, there exists a significant segment that views the terrorist group favorably. Anti-American sentiment is seen to be at peak levels within all spectra of Pakistani society, fueled by perceptions that the United States is fighting a war against Islam, that it is insufficiently attentive to the process of democratization in Pakistan, and that drone strikes and other U.S. operations on Pakistani territory are a violation of national sovereignty. A Pew Center public opinion survey released in July 2010 found the percentage of Pakistanis holding a favorable view of Al Qaeda doubling from 9% in 2009 to 18% in 2010. The poll also found only 17% of Pakistanis holding a favorable view of the United States; nearly three in five described the United States as "an enemy," while only 11% saw it as "a partner."[51]

A significant and long-term increase in economic and development assistance to Pakistan is a key aspect of the Obama Administration's effort to reduce the bilateral "trust deficit"—the Enhanced Partnership With Pakistan Act of 2009 (P.L. 111-73) authorized $1.5 billion in annual nonmilitary aid through FY2014. Moreover, the United States plans to continue devoting considerable resources toward bolstering Pakistan's counterterrorism and counterinsurgency capabilities (a new "Pakistan Counterterrorism Capability Fund" provided $1.1 billion for this cause in FY2009- FY2010). Yet U.S. troops are officially prohibited from operating on Pakistani territory, and the combination of distrust of Americans and a dire security environment makes it extremely difficult for U.S. officials to operate effectively there.

For the near and middle term, then, it appears that U.S. strategy likely will continue to rely on large-scale economic and development aid, redoubled efforts to build Pakistan's relevant military capacity, accelerated drone attacks on militant targets, and admonitions that Pakistani leaders consolidate what progress they have made and endeavor to keep pressure on Al Qaeda and its allies on their territory.

AL QAEDA IN THE ARABIAN PENINSULA (AQAP)[52]

Background and Threat Assessment

In January 2009, Al Qaeda-affiliated militants based in Yemen announced that Saudi militants had pledged allegiance to their leader and that the group would now operate under the banner of Al Qaeda in the Arabian Peninsula (AQAP).[53] A previous Saudi Arabia-based version of AQAP was largely dismantled and destroyed by Saudi security forces after a long and costly counterterrorism campaign from 2003 through 2007.[54] Some Saudi militants fled to Yemen to avoid death or capture, helping to lay the groundwork for a reemergence of the organization there in recent years alongside Al Qaeda figures who escaped from Yemeni custody and former Saudi detainees from Guantanamo Bay, Cuba and the Saudi terrorism rehabilitation program.

The emergence of Yemen as a safe haven for a reconstituted Al Qaeda threat has left Saudi officials working to prevent "inspiration and re-infiltration" by the new incarnation of AQAP. Continuing terrorism arrests have sustained concerns, particularly because of an apparent shift in attackers' objectives toward targeting critical energy infrastructure and Saudi government officials.[55] The arrest in Saudi Arabia of over 110 terrorist suspects in March 2010, along with reports that some of the suspects planned to target energy installations, highlighted these concerns. The attempted assassination of Assistant Interior Minister for Security Affairs Prince Mohammed bin Nayef bin Abdelaziz Al Saud in August 2009 underscored the threat to the royal family.[56] In 2010, AQAP leaders released an direct appeal to Saudi security and military personnel to turn their weapons on government officials and royal family members.[57] The recruitment of Saudis who have passed through the kingdom's terrorist rehabilitation program has raised new questions about the tactics employed in the program and underlying assumptions about the rehabilitation prospects for committed, violent Al Qaeda supporters.

Yemen is an attractive base of operations for AQAP. Unlike Saudi Arabia, Yemen's much poorer population is more disperse, rural, and geographically isolated than its neighbors. The central government, which is widely vilified for its poor governance and corruption, cannot exercise direct control in several of its own governorates without first seeking tribal support. President Ali Abdullah Saleh has ruled Yemen since its unification in 1990. Before that, Saleh ruled North Yemen from 1978 onward. He has a long history of allying himself with Sunni Islamist militants against Communist or Shiite[58] (revivalist

Zaydi[59]) domestic opponents. These ties have led in the past to his government's somewhat complacent attitude toward Al Qaeda sympathizers,[60] particularly when faced with other, more pressing security challenges in the north (Houthi conflict) and south (secessionist movement) that are perceived as more of a direct threat to Saleh's rule. As Yemen's oil production drops precipitously, its population rises, its water tables drop, and its government coffers dwindle, the country only becomes more ripe for instability and extremist activity.

AQAP operates both within the Arabian Peninsula and internationally. Some analysts also suggest that, with the encouragement of Al Qaeda leaders in Afghanistan and Pakistan, the group is expanding its ties with Al Shabaab in Somalia, though the extent of those ties is unknown. AQAP also may be working with other AQ affiliates. The *Washington Post* reported that France, with help from Saudi intelligence, recently broke up a joint AQAP-AQIM terrorist cell planning to carry out attacks inside France.[61]

Overall, AQAP seeks to:

- **Attack the U.S. homeland:** Most counter terrorism analysts believe that of all of Al Qaeda's regional affiliates, AQAP is the most active organization seeking to carry out a successful attack inside the United States.[62] As it has demonstrated both through Anwar al Awlaki's indoctrination of American citizens and the sophisticated bomb-making of Ibrahim Hassan al Asiri[63] and others, AQAP is trying to radicalize U.S. citizens and carry out an attention-grabbing terrorist bombing on U.S. soil. In the third edition of its online Inspire magazine released in November 2010, AQAP claims that the October 2010 air cargo bomb plot was part of a long-term strategy to launch many small-scale attacks against the United States. The group states that "This strategy of attacking the enemy with smaller but more frequent operations is what some may refer to as the strategy of a thousand cuts. The aim is to bleed the enemy to death....It is such a good bargain for us to spread fear amongst the enemy and keep him on his toes in exchange of a few months of work and a few thousand bucks....In such an environment of security phobia that is sweeping America it is more feasible to stage smaller attacks that involve less players and less time to launch and thus we may circumvent the security barriers American worked so hard to erect."[64]

- **Attack U.S. and Western Interests in Yemen:** Even before the Saudi-Yemeni merger, militants in Yemen have targeted Western Embassies in Sana'a, foreign oil companies and their facilities, and tourists. Two attacks on the U.S. Embassy in Sana'a in 2008 killed 17 people, including one U.S. citizen, and injured dozens of Yemenis. On April 26, 2010, AQAP carried out an unsuccessful assassination attempt against British Ambassador to Yemen Timothy Torlot, an operation that many experts believe was designed to demonstrate the group's resilience in the face of a government crackdown following the Christmas Day attempted bombing. In October 2010, AQAP gunmen attacked a vehicle carrying five British embassy workers in Sana'a. The attack injured one British worker and two Yemeni bystanders. Britain's second- ranking diplomat in Yemen, Fionna Gibb, was in the car, but escaped uninjured.
- **Destabilize the Yemeni Government:** Unlike previous generations of Islamist fighters in Yemen who fought elsewhere, such as in Afghanistan, many of AQAP's footsoldiers are more inclined to target the Yemeni government itself. Throughout much of 2010, AQAP's activities inside Yemen have resembled the kind of insurgent warfare witnessed most recently in Afghanistan, Pakistan, and Iraq. It appears that one of the group's goals is to use the popular hatred of the central government, particularly in the former areas of Southern Yemen, to fuel a popular insurgency that is capable of holding territory. To date, this strategy has succeeded in sowing a certain degree of chaos and violence in the provinces of Abyan and Shabwah, though many observers remain skeptical of AQAP's ability to evolve into a mass movement such as the Taliban. There is no indication that large numbers of Yemeni tribesmen are open to Al Qaeda's ideological appeal, and many tribal leaders may be using AQAP as a temporary lever to pressure the government for benefits, settle scores with rival, neighboring tribes, or to strike back against the government to avenge some perceived historical injustice.
- **Assassinate Members of the Saudi Royal Family:** Several of AQAP's top leaders are Saudi veterans combatants from conflicts involving Muslims in other regions or graduates of terrorist training camps based in Afghanistan who, upon returning home nearly a decade ago, turned inward against the Saudi royal family. Since their expulsion from the kingdom, they have used their positions within AQAP to strike back against the Saudi royal family, as was vividly

illustrated by a failed assassination attempt in August 2009 against Assistant Interior Minister Prince Mohammed bin Nayef bin Abdelaziz Al Saud, the director of the kingdom's counterterrorism campaign. According to one report, two of Saudi Arabia's most powerful intelligence agencies, the Saudi General Intelligence Presidency (GIP), headed since October 2005 by Prince Muqrin bin Abdulaziz, and the General Security Services (GSS), which is attached to the Saudi Interior Ministry, have been working with Yemen's military and special forces units. In the lead up to the October 2010 failed air cargo bombing, Bin Nayef reportedly provided John Brennan, the Deputy National Security Advisor for Homeland Security and Counterterrorism, and Assistant to the President with critical information on the plot reportedly derived from a Saudi informant or an AQAP member who had recently turned himself in to Saudi authorities.[65]

A Profile of Yemeni-American Terrorist Anwar Al Awlaki

Yemeni-American Anwar Al Awlaki (alt. sp. Aulaqi) was born in New Mexico in 1971, and he hails from a prominent tribal family in the southern governorate of Shabwa. Awlaki lived in Britain and in the United States, where he worked as an imam and lecturer at several mosques, including in Falls Church, VA. He traveled to Yemen in 2004, where he became a lecturer at Al Iman University. He was arrested by Yemeni authorities in 2006 and interrogated by the FBI in September 2007 for his possible contacts with some of the 9/11 hijackers. According to various reports, he began openly supporting the use of violence against the United States after his release from prison.

For the past several years, Awlaki has been one of the most deadly terrorist masterminds confronting the United States. He has been either directly or indirectly linked to radicalizing Major Nidal M. Hasan (allegedly committed the November 2009 mass shooting at Fort Hood Army Base in Texas), Umar Farouk Abdulmutallab (the Nigerian suspect accused of trying to ignite explosive chemicals to destroy Northwest/Delta Airlines Flight 253 from Amsterdam to Detroit on Christmas Day 2009), and Faisal Shahzad (alleged Times Square failed car bomb), who allegedly told U.S. investigators that Awlaki's online lectures urging jihad helped inspire him to act.

> According to several reports, the Obama Administration has added Awlaki, an American citizen, to the CIA's list of suspected terrorists who may be captured or killed. To date, Yemen has refused to extradite Awlaki (Article 44 of the Yemeni constitution states that a Yemeni national may not be extradited to a foreign authority), and his tribe has vowed to protect him. In January 2011, a Yemeni court sentenced Awlaki in absentia to ten years in prison on charges of incitement to murder and belonging to a terrorist group.

Implications for U.S. Policy

For the past several months, numerous reports have indicated the Obama Administration is contemplating how to properly increase assistance and intelligence cooperation with Yemen without overly militarizing the U.S. presence there and causing a backlash from the local population. Based on numerous reports, it appears that the Administration is simultaneously pursuing a short term decapitation strategy to capture or eliminate the top echelons of AQAP's leadership while also enacting policies over the long run to address the growing instability in Yemen that permits AQAP to grow.

In the short term, some reports suggest that the CIA may increase its use of drones inside Yemen or place military units overseen by the Defense Department (JSOC) under its control.[66] Anonymous U.S. officials have said that Predator drones (possibly launched from either Djibouti, Qatar, or the Seychelles Islands) have been patrolling the skies over Yemen in search of AQAP leaders, but many of these leaders have gone into hiding. One report suggests that a major buildup of U.S. assets is occurring in Yemen with the arrival of additional CIA teams and up to 100 Special Operations force trainers, and the deployment of sophisticated surveillance and electronic eavesdropping systems operated by spy services including the National Security Agency.[67] The U.S. military historically has maintained only a limited presence in Yemen, and as such, U.S. intelligence agencies may have limited knowledge of the local terrain and may need time before they are able to effectively employ all assets to their maximum capacity. On November 8, an anonymous senior Administration official said that the White House was pushing the Yemeni government for more collaboration and intelligence sharing.[68]

In the long term, the Administration has significantly increased U.S. economic and military aid, although Yemen's socio-economic challenges far exceed current U.S. and international development efforts. In FY2010, the United States is providing an estimated $290 million in total aid and that figure is expected to increase in FY2011. The Defense Department also has proposed increasing its Section 1206 security assistance to Yemen to $1.2 billion over a five-or six-year period.[69] In the past, the Yemeni government has cautioned the United States against overreacting to the terrorist threat there, though in recent months, Yemeni forces have launched several large-scale campaigns against suspected AQAP strongholds in the Abyan and Shabwah governorates.

Whether U.S.-Yemeni security cooperation can be sustained over the long term is the key question for U.S. lawmakers and policymakers. Inevitably, at some point, disagreements arise over Yemen's tendency to release alleged terrorists from prison in order to placate tribal leaders and domestic Islamist politicians who oppose U.S. "interference" in Yemen and U.S. policy in the region in general. One report suggests that in the fall of 2009, U.S. officials met with President Saleh and showed him "irrefutable evidence that Al Qaeda was aiming at him and his relatives," and "that seems to have abruptly changed Saleh's attitude."[70] At times, the United States government itself shares the blame for limiting its bilateral cooperation with Yemen. In the past, high-level U.S. policymakers have shifted focus to what have appeared to be more pressing counterterrorism fronts or areas of the Middle East. Yemeni leaders have grown adept at sensing U.S. interest and have adjusted their level of cooperation accordingly. According to Abdel-Karim al Iryani, a former prime minister, "The trust between the U.S. and Yemen comes and goes.... Everyone has his own calculations on what they want from this relationship."[71]

NORTH AFRICA/SAHEL: AL QAEDA IN THE ISLAMIC MAGHREB (AQIM)[72]

Background and Threat Assessment

Al Qaeda in the Islamic Maghreb (AQIM, also known as Al Qaeda in the Lands of the Islamic Maghreb or AQLIM) and its offshoots or autonomous cells pose the main terrorist threat in North Africa and the Sahel. Under pressure from Algerian security forces, AQIM has increasingly moved its operations out of the Algerian capital of Algiers. The vast area of Algeria's six Saharan provinces and of its sparsely populated Sahelian neighbors affords AQIM optimal terrain in which to move and conduct training as well as to advance its regional ambitions. Algeria's North African neighbors, Tunisia and Morocco, have prevented AQIM from penetrating their territories, except for some recruitment of individuals; both governments fear that AQIM will transfer operational capabilities to indigenous groups. Neither has experienced a major terrorism attack for several years, but both governments and that of Mauritania continue to unearth alleged Al Qaeda cells and affiliated terrorists.

It is not clear what AQIM's "unity" with or "allegiance" to Al Qaeda means in practice as the group does not appear to take directions from leaders in Afghanistan/Pakistan. A nominal link is probably mutually beneficial, burnishing Al Qaeda's international credentials as it enhances AQIM's legitimacy among radicals to facilitate recruitment. Since "uniting" with Al Qaeda in 2006, AQIM's rhetoric against the West and governments in the region and beyond (e.g., to Nigeria) as well as its calls for *jihad* against the United States, France, and Spain have increased. Yet, its operations remain geographically limited to Algeria and the Sahel, and public information available does not suggest a direct AQIM threat to the U.S. homeland. In mid-2010, French officials declared that France is "at war Al Qaeda" following AQIM's murder of a French hostage and AQIM issued several calls for attacks on France. A French national critical terrorism threat alert in September 2010 was attributed, in part, to a rise in AQIM threats, and in October, a message attributed to Osama Bin Laden justified AQIM and other Al Qaeda attacks on France.[73]

Algeria

AQIM's origins date to the 1990s, when Islamist extremists and security forces engaged in a conflict sparked by a 1992 military coup that prevented an Islamist political party from winning a national election in Algeria. The terrorists sought (and seek) to replace the Algerian regime with an Islamic state. The Armed Islamic Group (GIA) was then the main terrorist threat.[74] In 1998, the Salafist Group for Preaching and Combat (GSPC) split from GIA, claiming to oppose the GIA's indiscriminate targeting of civilians. In 2003, under new leader Abdelmalik Droukdel (aka Abu Musab Abdulwadood), GSPC declared "allegiance" to Al Qaeda. In 2006, it announced "unity" with Al Qaeda, changing its name to Al Qaeda in the Islamic Maghreb. AQIM raises funds by kidnapping for ransom and by trafficking arms, drugs, vehicles, cigarettes, and persons, and receives small-scale funding from cells in Europe.[75] AQIM communicates via sophisticated online videos.

In 2006, AQIM increased its attacks against the government, security forces, and foreign workers in Algeria. In 2007, it shifted tactics to "Iraqi-style," suicide attacks, with simultaneous bombings of the Government Palace (the prime and interior ministries) and a suburban police station in April, and of the Constitutional Council and the U.N. headquarters in December, among other attacks. An AQIM suicide bomber failed to assassinate President Abdelaziz Bouteflika in September. After a relative lull, terrorist attacks on security forces escalated in summer 2008, when suicide bombers perpetrated a particularly bloody attack at a police academy, resulting in more than 40 deaths. In 2009, perhaps because security forces had made it difficult to conduct operations in the capital, AQIM mounted attacks elsewhere, notably in the Berber region of the Kabylie in northeastern Algeria, where the security presence had been reduced to pacify civil unrest, although it also shifted its attacks elsewhere.[76] In June, gunmen killed 24 gendarmes (paramilitary police) in an ambush more than 200 miles east Algiers. In July, they ambushed a military convoy 90 miles west of Algiers, killing at least 14 soldiers.[77] In 2010, AQIM continued carry out attacks on police, including in areas outside the northeast.[78]

Several Al Qaeda-linked international terrorist plots have involved Algerians. In December 1999, Ahmed Ressam, an Algerian trained in Afghanistan, was arrested after attempting to enter the United States from Canada; he was convicted for the so-called Millennium Plot that planned bombings in Los Angeles. His associates and other Algerians in Canada were linked to the GIA and Al Qaeda. In January 2003, six Algerians were arrested in a London apartment with traces of ricin, a deadly poison with no known antidote. In October 2009, two French brothers of Algerian origin, one a worker at the European Organization for Nuclear Research (CERN) in Geneva, were arrested in France after intelligence agencies came to suspect them of "criminal activities related to a terror group" (i.e., AQIM).[79] Algeria continues to be a major source of international terrorists, and Algerians have been arrested on suspicion of belonging to or supporting AQIM in France, Spain, Italy, Germany, and Britain.

The Sahel

AQIM has become increasingly active in the West African Sahel, where it "continues to demonstrate its intent and ability to conduct attacks against U.S. citizens or other foreign nationals," according to the State Department.[80] The

Sahel stretches from Mauritania to Chad and encompasses several poor, often politically unstable countries with large, sparsely populated northern border areas and limited state capacity to monitor or secure them. AQIM reportedly maintains mobile training camps along the Algeria-Mali border, and carries out smuggling operations in countries across the Sahel, taking advantage of porous international borders. The group has carried out raids on military and police targets, primarily in Mauritania and Mali; kidnapped or assassinated tourists, diplomats, and private sector workers in these countries; carried out kidnappings in Niger; attacked foreign embassies in Mauritania; and repeatedly clashed with the militaries of Mali, Mauritania, Niger, and Algeria.

In 2007, AQIM associates murdered four French tourists, prompting cancelation of the famous Dakar Motor Rally. In 2008, AQIM assassinated 12 Mauritanian soldiers and kidnapped a U.N. envoy to Niger and a Canadian colleague. The Canadians and several European tourists kidnapped in early 2009 were held in Mali and released several months later. A Briton in the group was beheaded after his government refused to meet AQIM demands to release a radical cleric with alleged Al Qaeda ties. In June 2009, a U.S. aid worker in Mauritania was murdered in an apparent kidnapping attempt for which AQIM claimed credit and, in August, AQIM carried out a suicide bombing near the French embassy in Nouakchott, Mauritania. In June 2009, it also assassinated a Malian military official involved in the arrest of several AQIM members. That killing was followed by a series of armed clashes between AQIM and Malian forces, which, with Algerian military aid and French air intelligence support, vowed an "all-out war" on AQIM. The threat of kidnapping is of growing concern. In November 2009, a heavily armed group attempted unsuccessfully to kidnap U.S. embassy employees in Niger and, in June 2010, U.S. embassies in the Sahel warned U.S. citizens of prospective AQIM kidnapping operation in the Mali-NigerBurkina Faso border region. In July 2010, a Mauritanian-French attempt to rescue a French hostage in Mali resulted in AQIM fatalities, but the hostage was not secured and his death was announced days later. In August 2010, two kidnapped Spanish aid workers were released.[81] In late August 2010, a suicide attack on a Mauritanian military post, attributed to AQIM, was thwarted. In mid-September 2010, seven French uranium mine workers were kidnapped in Niger and then moved into Mali. Days later, Mauritania launched "pre-emptive" air raids in Mali that reportedly killed several AQIM combatants but also civilians.

AQIM's presence in the Sahel is divided between two main groups, one led by Yahia Djouadi and a second by Mokhtar Belmokhtar (MBM). The groups' members are primarily Algerian, but include individuals from Mauritania, Niger, Mali as well as Senegal, Ghana, Nigeria, and Benin.[82] The groups appear to cooperate operationally, but their roles and relations are not clear. Differences between them may be reflected in the outcomes of the kidnappings noted above: in two cases, hostages were executed, reportedly after AQIM political demands were not met, while all other hostages were released, reportedly by MBM in return for ransom.[83] While terrorist attacks are attributed to MBM's group, its activities focus on criminal income-earning operations, including kidnappings for ransom. It reportedly maintains a regional network of contacts, including state officials, possibly marking it as relatively pragmatic compared to other AQIM elements.

Implications for U.S. Policy

U.S. policy makers' efforts to assist North African and Sahelian governments in countering AQIM threats may need to take into account colonial history and regional power balances and navigate them adroitly. Algeria, Mauritania, Niger, and Mali are all former colonies of France and often resist foreign involvement in their internal affairs and territories. Algeria, which waged a bloody independence war against France, is particularly opposed to foreign interference. It has a stronger military and is richer than its neighbors, thanks to its oil and gas wealth, and sees itself as a dominant regional power. Relations between Algeria and other AQIM-affected Sahelian countries have sometimes been strained due to Algeria's regional aspirations and attempts to act as the key U.S. regional interlocutor and prevent French interference in the region. However, efforts to strengthen regional counterterrorism capabilities are being pursued via a variety of U.S. and European security cooperation programs and local initiatives. Algeria has hosted regional counterterrorism meetings, provided air cover for some Sahelian counterterrorist operations, and provided military aid to Mali and Niger. Under a 2010 agreement, the Tamanrasset Plan, Algeria, Mali, Mauritania and Niger are establishing a joint military center to combat terrorism, kidnappings, and trafficking. Under the plan, Algeria is to provide military materiel to other plan participants, and the latter are to expand the size of their militaries.

The U.S. government has conducted several initiatives to counter violent extremism in the region. In 2002, the State Department launched the Pan-Sahel Initiative (PSI) to increase border security, and military and counterterrorism capacities of Chad, Niger, Mali, and Mauritania. PSI programs focused solely on building security sector capacity. In 2005, the Bush Administration announced a "follow-on" program known as the Trans Sahara Counterterrorism Partnership (TSCTP). An inter-agency, multi-faceted effort, TSCTP integrates counterterrorism and military training with development assistance and public diplomacy. It aims to improve "individual country and regional capabilities to defeat terrorist organizations [by ...] disrupting efforts to recruit and train new terrorists, particularly from the young and rural poor, and countering efforts to establish safe havens for ... extremist groups."[84] TSCTP is led by the State Department, but other agencies, including the U.S. Agency for International Development and the Department of Defense (DOD), implement components of the program, including DOD's Operation Enduring Freedom—TransSahara (OEF-TS).[85] Under OEF-TS, U.S. military forces work with African counterparts to improve intelligence, command and control, logistics, and border control, and to execute joint operations against terrorist groups.[86]

Governments in the Sahel, a region where democratic gains have often been limited, face diverse security threats, including armed insurrection, banditry, illegal trafficking, and other criminal activities that may threaten state stability more directly than Islamist terrorism. Some in the development community question whether U.S. policy toward the region strikes an appropriate balance between countering extremism and addressing basic challenges of governance, security, and human development, which some view as contributing to the rise of extremism. Others question whether the U.S. response employs the appropriate mix of civilian and military resources or employs a counterproductive "militarization" of U.S. foreign policy in the region.

EAST AFRICA[87]

Background and Threat Assessment

The East Africa region has emerged over the past two decades as a region highly vulnerable to terrorist attacks and is considered a safe haven for international terrorist groups. Africa's porous borders, lax security at airports and seaports, and weak law enforcement agencies are major concerns. Political, ethnic, and religious conflicts in the region help create an environment conducive to the growth of and recruitment capabilities of terrorist groups. The inability of African security services to detect and intercept terrorist activities due to lack of technology and sufficiently trained and motivated manpower are major impediments addressing the terrorist threats in Africa.

The takeover of power in Sudan by the National Islamic Front (NIF) in 1989 led to a significant increase in the activities of international terror groups in Africa. The NIF government provided safe haven for well known international terrorist organizations and individuals, and the government's security services also were directly engaged in facilitating and assisting domestic and international terror groups. Sudan has also been a safe haven for major terrorist figures, including the founder and leader of Al Qaeda, Osama Bin Laden. Bin Laden used Sudan as a base of operations until he returned to Afghanistan in mid-1996, where he had previously been a major financier of Arab volunteers in the war against the Soviet occupation of Afghanistan.

Many observers contend that it was during his five-year stay in Sudan that Bin Laden laid down the foundation for Al Qaeda. The penetration by Al Qaeda into East Africa is directly tied to NIF's early years of support to international terrorist organizations. The East Africa region is by far the most impacted by international terrorist activities in Africa. The 1990s saw dramatic and daring terrorist attacks against American interests in Africa. The U.S. Embassy bombings in Kenya and Tanzania in 1998 by Al Qaeda killed 229 people, 12 of whom were American citizens, and injured over 5,000 people. In November, 2002, simultaneous terrorist attacks struck Mombasa, Kenya. Al Qaeda suicide bombers drove a four-wheel drive vehicle packed with explosives into the Israeli-owned Paradise Hotel in Mombasa, killing 10 Kenyans and three Israelis. In June 1995, members of Gama'a Islamiya, an Egyptian extremist group, tried to assassinate President Hosni Mubarak of Egypt in Addis Ababa, Ethiopia.

On July 11, 2010, the Somali terrorist group Al Shabaab carried out multiple suicide bombings in Kampala, Uganda. An estimated 76 people, including one American, were killed and more than 80 injured. The United Nations, the African Union, and the United States condemned the terrorist attacks. The attacks took place at a rugby club and Ethiopian restaurant while people were watching the final match of the World Cup. The following day, an Al Shabaab official, Ali Mohamud Rage, stated that "we are sending a message to Uganda and Burundi, if they do not take out their AMISOM troops from Somalia, blasts will continue and it will happen in Bujumbura (Burundi's capital)."[88]

Al Shabaab and the Islamist Movements in Somalia

The United States, Somalia's neighbors, and some Somali groups have expressed concern over the years about the spread of Islamic fundamentalism in Somalia. In the mid-1990s, Islamic courts emerged in parts of the country, especially in the capital of Mogadishu. These courts functioned as local governments and often enforced decisions by using their own militia. Members of the Al Ittihad Al Islami[89] militia reportedly provided the bulk of the security forces for these courts in the 1990s. The absence of central authority in Somalia created an environment conducive to the proliferation of armed factions throughout the country. Somali factions, including the so-called Islamist groups, often go through realignments or simply disappear from the scene. In late September 2001, the Bush Administration added Al Ittihad to a list of terrorism-related entities whose assets were frozen by an Executive Order 13224. Bush Administration officials accused Al Ittihad Al Islami of links with Al Qaeda. The leader of Hizbul Islam, Sheikh Hassan Aweys, who is on the U.S. terrorist list, was a leader in Al Ittihad Al Islami. In the late 1990s, after Ethiopia and its Somali allies attacked and crushed Al Ittihad, a number of its fighters, the current leadership of Al Shabaab, went to Afghanistan and others went underground.

The Evolution of Al Shabaab[90]

In 2003, the leadership of Al Ittihad, including Sheik Ali Warsame, brother in law of Sheik Hassan Aweys and a number of other top leaders, decided to form a new political front. The young members of Al Ittihad disagreed with the decision of the older leadership in 2003 and decided to form their own movement. These young leaders, some of whom had fought in Afghanistan, met in Laasa aanood, a town in northern Somalia, and later formed a group known then as Harakat Al Shabaab Al Mujahedeen, currently known as Al Shabaab. The current leader of Al Shabaab, Ahmed Abdi Godane, the late Aden Hashi Ayrow, Ibrahim Haji Jama, Mukhtar Robow, helped form the new movement. The primary objective of this group was irredentism and to establish a "Greater Somalia" under Sharia. But Al Shabaab was not active and did not control any territory in Somalia until 2007-2008.

The Ethiopian invasion and the ouster of the Courts from power in December 2006 contributed to the emergence of a strong resistance movement. The leadership of the Islamic Courts moved to Eritrea, while the Al Shabaab secretive leadership slowly took control over the resistance movement. Many Somalis joined the fight against the Ethiopian forces. Some of these volunteers did not know or had only limited knowledge of the intent and objectives of Al Shabaab. By mid-2007, the true leaders of Al Shabaab emerged and the ties with Al-Qaeda became clear. In February 2008, then Secretary of State Condoleezza Rice designated Al Shabaab as a Foreign Terrorist Organization and as a Specially Designated Global Terrorist.

Al Shabaab and Other Somali Terrorist Groups in Somalia

On February 1, 2010, Al Shabaab and the Ras Kamboni group, led by Hassan Al Turki, reportedly agreed to merge under one name: Al Shabaab Mujahidin Movement. Both Al Shabaab and the Ras Kamboni group have been coordinating their attacks against Somalia's Transitional Federal Government (TFG) and working closely with Al Qaeda leaders in East Africa and foreign fighters over the past three years. Senior TFG officials consider the merger a reaffirmation of a preexisting informal alliance between the two groups.[91] The merger is also triggered in part due to defections and the reported illness of Hassan Al Turki, the leader of Ras Kamboni. Al Turki, an Ethiopian from the Ogaden clan, was designated as a terrorist by the United States in 2004. In December 2010, Hizbul Islam merged with Al Shabaab. The merger is seen by some observers as a surrender after a string of defeats on the ground.

Implications for U.S. Policy[92]

Al Qaeda poses a direct threat against U.S. interests and allies in East Africa. Al Shabaab, on the other hand, appears more focused on carrying out attacks against Somali citizens, the TFG, and African Union peacekeeping forces (AMISOM). According to the 2010 *State Department Country Reports on Terrorism*, "Al-Shabaab's leadership was supportive of al-Qa'ida (AQ), and both groups continued to present a serious terrorist threat to American and allied interests throughout the Horn of Africa." On February 2, 2010, Director of National Intelligence Dennis Blair at a Senate Select Committee on Intelligence hearing stated:

> We judge most Al Shabaab and East Africa-based Al Qaeda members will remain focused on regional objectives in the near-term. Nevertheless, East Africa-based Al Qaeda leaders or Al Shabaab may elect to redirect to the Homeland some of the Westerners, including North Americans, now training and fighting in Somalia.[93]

Reportedly, over a dozen Somali youth from Minneapolis and other parts of the United States have left the country, and some community leaders believe they went to Somalia to join the insurgency. There is no clear evidence of how many and for what purpose these Somalis left Minneapolis, although some U.S. counterterrorism officials have expressed concern to Congress that some of these individuals could be recruited by Al Qaeda to perform attacks in Somalia or the United States.[94] U.S. officials stressed in early 2009 that they did not possess "credible reporting" that suggested such an operation targeting the U.S. homeland was planned or imminent.[95] The concerns appear based in part on the fact that one of the suicide bombers in the October 2008 attacks in Puntland and Somaliland was a Somali-American from Minneapolis, although broader concerns exist about the participation of U.S. citizens in Al Shabaab activities and potential U.S.-based financing for terrorist groups in Somalia. Over the past decade, many Somalis have returned to Somalia to work as journalists, humanitarian workers, and teachers. A number of these Somalis have been killed in the past two years by insurgents and security forces.

On August 5, 2010, more than a dozen Somali-Americans/permanent residents were indicted in California, Alabama, and Minnesota. Attorney General Eric Holder announced that 14 people are being charged with providing support to Al Shabaab. Two indictments unsealed in Minnesota state that Amina Farah Ali and Hawo Mohamed Hassan raised funds for Al Shabaab. The indictments state that 12 money transfers were made in 2008 and 2009. Holder stated at a press conference that "the indictments unsealed today shed further light on a deadly pipeline that has routed funding and fighters to the Al Shabaab terror organization from cities across the United States. These arrests and charges should serve as an unmistakable warning to others considering joining terrorist groups like Al Shabaab—if you choose this route, you can expect to find yourself in a U.S. jail cell or a casualty on the battlefield in Somalia."

AL QAEDA AND RADICAL ISLAMIST EXTREMISTS IN SOUTHEAST ASIA[96]

Background and Threat Assessment

The United States and Indonesia have a common interest in addressing the threat of militant Islamists in Indonesia and Southeast Asia. The syncretic nature of Islam in Indonesia, which has overlaid earlier animist, Buddhist, and Hindu traditions, is more moderate in character than Islam is in the Middle East or Pakistan. Further, the main political parties in Indonesia are secular-nationalist in their outlook. However, radical or militant Islamists are a threat to the largely secular state and moderate Muslim society of Indonesia. Terrorist activity is not limited to attacking Western targets in Indonesia. In June 2010, one militant was sentenced for his role in a plan to assassinate President Yudhoyono as well as for his involvement in two hotel bombings in Jakarta in 2009.[97]

Indonesian views of the nature of the threat from militant Islamists have evolved over time. Islamists were generally suppressed under the New Order regime of former President Suharto. The *reformasi* period that followed Suharto's fall allowed an opening up of society that gave such views space that was absent under the New Order. After the 2002 Bali bombing that killed over 200 people, Indonesia moved from seeing local militant Islamist groups, such as Jemaah Islamiya (JI), as threats not only to Western and American interests in Indonesia but also as direct threats to the Indonesian government and the Indonesian people. Key terrorist attacks in Indonesia include the Bali bombing of 2002, the 2003 bombing of the Marriott Hotel in Jakarta, the 2004 bombing of the Australian Embassy, and bombing attacks against Western hotels in Jakarta in 2009.

While for most of the 2000s, JI was the key terrorist organization in Indonesia, this now appears to be shifting. According to Sidney Jones of the International Crisis Group, it now appears that militant Islamists can be identified with one of three groups: JI; the remaining members of the network of Noordin Top, a militant killed in 2009; and a new alliance of various Jihadists that had set up a training camp in Aceh. JI is evidently now focused on rebuilding its organization after having been effectively pursued by the Indonesian government. JI is also focused on establishing an Islamist state in Indonesia and possibly the region, as opposed to the Noordin Top network that is more focused on attacking Western targets in Indonesia.

The raid on the new alliance of Jihadists in Aceh, which began on February 22, 2010, has uncovered a group which according to Sydney Jones "...is a composite of people from a number of different militant groups like Jemaah Islamiya, Kompak and Darul Islam, who are frustrated with what they see as a lack of action within these groups. They're more radical, and apparently see themselves as Indonesia's Al Qaeda."[98] The February Aceh raid apparently led to the March 2010 raid that killed a militant named Dulmatin, who is thought to be one of the planners and executers of the 2002 Bali bombing. It is thought that a militant named Saptono took over the Aceh cell after Dulmatin was killed. Saptono was in turn killed during a raid in May 2010.[99] Some experts have observed that the capture, rather than the killing, of such leaders could yield valuable intelligence.

In May 2010, it was reported that a plot to assassinate President Yudhoyono and other national leaders in a rifle/grenade attack on Indonesia's Independence day (August 17, 2010) was disrupted. It was also reported that the plotters were considering moving the attack up to coincide with President Obama's now canceled June 2010 visit.[100] A leader of the Aceh cell that was reportedly planning to assassinate President Yudhoyono, Abdullah Sunata, was captured in June, 2010. He was previously released from prison after having been imprisoned for his role in the Australian embassy bombing.[101]

The government's response to militant Islamists has been largely effective, though there are some problem areas. Rivalry between the Indonesian military (TNI), the police, and the state intelligence agency BIN probably keeps the state's response from being as effective as it could be. Lax standards at prisons have reportedly allowed militants to communicate with their organizations while in prison. Government-run deradicalization programs, which are more cooptative than ideological in nature, have reportedly allowed some militants to rejoin their organizations after their release from prison.[102] Indonesia has reportedly arrested 400 terror suspects and released 242.[103]

In September 2010, General Ansyaad Mbai was appointed head of Indonesia's new National Counter Terrorism Agency (BNPT) that was formed by presidential decree. The BNPT will carry out its functions under the Coordinating Minister of Security, Political and Legal Affairs and is tasked with formulating policies and programmes and coordinating the implementation of policies.[104] Some fears have been voiced that the BNPT will act in ways similar to former President Suharto's New Order regime. Others are concerned that BNPT may find it difficult to effectively coordinate the counter terror efforts of the police, TNI, and BIN.[105] Security Affairs Minister Djoko Suyanto stated that there was no room for complacency during his remarks to a BNPT organized conference on Counter Terrorism in October 2010.[106] Another new development in Indonesia's counter-terror operations in 2010 includes the use of TNI troops, particularly Kopassus troops, in counter-terror operations.[107]

There reportedly was an increase in low level terrorism activity in Indonesia in 2010 which appears to be aimed at building up terrorist groups financial resources. In the Fall of 2010 there were a number of robberies that were believed to be linked to efforts to fund radical organizations. Three policemen were killed at the Hamparan Perak police station a few days after police arrested robbers of a bank in Medan. Police killed three who robbed a bank in Padang.[108] The Indonesian police reportedly believe that Abu Bakar Ba'asyir delivered sermons in Medan which motivated the attacks on the Hamparan police station and the robbery of the Bank in Medan.[109]

Implications for U.S. Policy

The policy implications of developments in Indonesia are largely positive. Indonesia has moved from a somewhat ambivalent counter terror partner in the immediate post 9-11 period to a now effective, and increasingly close, partner. The evolving counter terror cooperation has also helped foster the larger bilateral relationship. President Obama, who spent part of his childhood in Indonesia, and President Susilo Bambang Yudhoyono signed a Comprehensive Partnership agreement during President Obama's visit to Indonesia in 2010. This marks a strengthening and broadening of U.S. relations with Indonesia and opens the way for developing closer strategic relations with Indonesia.

AL QAEDA'S GLOBAL STRATEGY AND IMPLICATIONS FOR U.S. POLICY[110]

Overall, Al Qaeda leaders' statements from the mid-1990s through the present suggest that they see themselves and their followers as the armed vanguard of an international Islamist movement. Nevertheless, some experts now argue that "al-Qa'ida has been a marginal actor in the larger drama of international Islamist militancy," and that believe that the group's "quest for influence has been in vain."[111] Al Qaeda and many of its affiliates state a commitment to ending non-Muslim "interference" in the affairs of Muslims and to recasting predominantly Muslim societies according to narrow interpretations derived from the practices of Sunni Islam's earliest generations. Statements from some Al Qaeda leaders advocate for a phased struggle, in which the initial goal is the expulsion of U.S. and foreign military forces from "Islamic lands" and proximate goals include the overthrow of "corrupt" regional leaders and the creation of governments that rule solely according sharia (Islamic law). References to the reestablishment of an Islamic caliphate frequently appear in Al Qaeda propaganda but often lack detail and are rarely accompanied by practical political prescriptions for achieving such a goal. Some Al Qaeda leaders also promote military confrontation with Israel and conflict with Shiite Muslims. The varying appeal and compatibility of these different components of Al Qaeda's ideology account for the group's successes and failures in attracting support.

In pursuit of their many goals, leaders of Al Qaeda and its regional affiliates frequently make appeals for support based on a wide range of political positions and, at times, attempt to harness nationalist sentiment or manipulate local grievances to generate support for their agendas. These differing priorities, approaches, and contexts create challenges for those Al Qaeda figures who have hoped to construct a unified narrative of Al Qaeda's goals or implement a unified strategy to achieve them. Some experts note that Al Qaeda's "description of the enemy is confusing and inconsistent" and suggest that, overall:

> "speaking of al-Qa'ida's "strategy" is a misnomer. The jihadi movement's various operational units, whether named al-Qa'ida affiliates or small cells, cull through various ideological and strategic documents to identify elements that they can achieve. Such strategic variation is enhanced by jihadis' inability to coordinate closely, which likely limits their ability to achieve ultimate policy goals, but also complicates the processes to combat the movement writ large."[112]

Although Osama Bin Laden's self-professed goal has been to "move, incite, and mobilize the [Islamic] nation" until it reaches a revolutionary "ignition point," Al Qaeda leaders' statements and Al Qaeda attacks to date appear largely to have failed to mobilize broad support among Muslims.[113] Some observers believe that Al Qaeda faces fundamental limits to its appeal because its rhetoric and goals extend beyond what many Muslims view as religiously legitimate or practically desirable.[114]

While global public opinion polls and media monitoring indicate that dissatisfaction with U.S. foreign policy has grown significantly in some predominantly Muslim societies, the sectarian rhetoric of some Al Qaeda affiliates and the persistence of Al Qaeda-inspired terrorist attacks that kill and maim Sunni and Shiite Muslim civilians have undermined Al Qaeda's appeal among some Muslim groups. Some experts also argue that the uncompromising, anti-democratic tone of many of the statements released by Bin Laden,

Al Zawahiri, and their regional supporters may be alienating Muslims who support the concept of secular or religious representative government.

Analysis of the statements issued by Al Qaeda leaders and affiliates since the mid-1990s suggests that these groups and individuals believe that characterizing their actions as religiously sanctioned, defensive reactions to external threats will increase tolerance of and support for their broader ideological program. Al Qaeda and its regional affiliates also appear to believe that the identification of limited political objectives and the suggestion to non-Muslim audiences that the fulfillment of those objectives will resolve their grievances may generate broader appeal than the group's underlying religious agenda. In fact, experts note that Al Qaeda and its affiliates "pursue a variety of objectives that are rarely clearly defined" and point out that the group "advocates everything from reestablishing the caliphate to the personal religious salvation of its members."[115] The practical political and operational realities facing many Al Qaeda affiliates in pursuit of their discrete goals and needs have often led these groups to take actions that have undermined their efforts to portray themselves as defenders of Muslims with limited objectives. For example:

- In December 2004, Bin Laden identified the conflict in Iraq as "a golden and unique opportunity" for jihadists to engage and defeat the United States, and he characterized the insurgency in Iraq as the central battle in a "Third World War, which the Crusader-Zionist coalition began against the Islamic nation." Nevertheless, several strategic choices made by Al Qaeda's affiliates in Iraq undermined their support among key groups, specifically their decisions to stoke sectarian conflict, to rigidly enforce religious doctrine in some areas, and to target the leaders and citizens of some Sunni Muslim communities. Each of these decisions contributed to the significant attrition the group has suffered from 2007 onward at the hands of Iraqi security forces, the government's Sunni allies among the Awakening and Sons of Iraq movements, and the United States military.
- Similarly, affiliates of Al Qaeda in Saudi Arabia initially oriented their attacks against foreign interests in the kingdom during their 2003-2007 campaign, in line with Al Qaeda leaders' rhetoric that had long targeted the U.S. military presence and other outside influences. Saudi security officials believe that once local Al Qaeda affiliates shifted the focus of their attacks away from foreign targets and onto

local security forces, Al Qaeda created an opportunity for the government to directly engage and eliminate the group. In addition to carrying out more robust security operations, the government launched a campaign that used nationalist sentiment to undermine popular support for the group by highlighting Al Qaeda attacks against security officers. Deradicalization programs have successfully demobilized some supporters of Al Qaeda, while other individuals have returned to militancy and rejected pro-government clerics' arguments about requiring rulers' and parents' permission to participate in violent jihad.

- Since 2006, Al Shabaab fighters in Somalia who affiliate themselves with Al Qaeda have rallied support from some Somalis opposed to external intervention in Somalia and the Transitional Federal Government (TFG). However, Al Shabaab threats against the United Nations World Food Program (WFP) and several other aid agencies have largely shut down humanitarian aid delivery in southern Somalia, cutting access to almost half of WFP's planned beneficiaries in 2010 and exacerbating food insecurity. Terror attacks against civilian targets, including a medical school graduation ceremony in late 2009 and a Mogadishu hotel in August 2010, also have served to alienate many Somalis. Amid recruiting efforts that have drawn ethnic Somalis and other foreigners from the United States and Europe to Somalia, Al Shabaab nevertheless has sought to publicly downplay the presence of foreign fighters within its ranks, given local sensitivities to foreigners using Somalia for their own purposes.
- In Southeast Asia, the Jemaah Islamiyah (JI) network's 2002 bomb attack in Bali, Indonesia that killed over 200 people led the Indonesian government to reverse course and undertake a concerted effort to track, arrest, and kill JI leaders, as well as to increase anti-terrorist cooperation with the United States and Australia. The ensuing crackdown in Indonesia and other countries appears to have degraded JI's capabilities, particularly its more militant factions, which were most closely associated with Al Qaeda. Since the mid-2000s, JI appears to be taking direction from more "bureaucratic" elements that oppose the militants' violent tactics, at least in the short term.

Many observers argue that the success or failure of U.S. and allied counterterrorism efforts are tied to decisions made by regional governments and publics about the relative importance of combating Al Qaeda operatives, affiliates, and ideologues within their own societies. Recent events suggest that U.S. and allied counterterrorism policies can be successful when they capitalize on Al Qaeda actions and messages that alienate current or potential supporters. Similarly, events also suggest that Al Qaeda members seek to capitalize on U.S. and allied policies and actions that are unpopular among Muslim audiences, such as military operations that result in civilian casualties as well as broader policies such as the presence of foreign military forces in Muslim countries. Action taken by the United States and its allies against Al Qaeda affiliates has the potential to shape the global fortunes of the Al Qaeda brand and the appeal of violent Islamism, and vice versa. Counterterrorism approaches that work in one theater of operations or political context may prove counterproductive when applied elsewhere. These complex dynamics and calculations are likely to continue to challenge decision makers and require unique approaches in each of the regional contexts described above.

End Notes

[1] Prepared by John Rollins, Specialist in Terrorism and National Security, ext. 7-5529.

[2] "U.S. Counterterrorism Policy," Remarks by Robert F. Godec, Principal Deputy Coordinator for Counterterrorism, State Department, speech at the Global Young Leaders Conference, June 30, 2010.

[3] "Testimony of Michael Leiter, Director of National Counterterrorism Center, hearing "Nine Years After 9/11: Confronting the Terrorist Threat to the Homeland," before the U.S. Senate Homeland Security and Governmental Affairs Committee, September 22, 2010.

[4] See comments of Brynjar Lia, an al Qaeda expert, in Ian Black and Richard Norton-Taylor, "Al-Qaida Faces Recruitment Crisis, Anti-terrorism Experts Say," *The Guardian*, September 10, 2009.

[5] "Annual Threat Assessment of the Intelligence Community for the Senate Select Committee on Intelligence," Dennis C. Blair, Director of National Intelligence, February 2, 2010.

[6] Ibid.

[7] See the text box on page 4 for a discussion of the use of the term jihad.

[8] "Annual Threat Assessment of the Intelligence Community for the Senate Select Committee on Intelligence," Dennis C. Blair, Director of National Intelligence, February 2, 2010.

[9] For information on attempted terrorist attacks occurring in the homeland in 2009 and 2010 see CRS Report R 41416, *American Jihadist Terrorism: Combating a Complex Threat*, by Jerome Bjelopera and Mark Randol.

[10] Testimony of Robert Mueller, "Nine Years After 9/11: Confronting the Terrorist Threat to the Homeland" before the U.S. Senate Committee on Homeland Security and Government Affairs, September 22, 2010.

[11] Testimony of Janet Napolitano, "Nine Years After 9/11: Confronting the Terrorist Threat to the Homeland" before the U.S. Senate Committee on Homeland Security and Government Affairs, September 22, 2010.

[12] Assaf Moghadam and Brian Fishman (eds.), *Self-Inflicted Wounds: Debates and Divisions within Al Qaeda and its Periphery*, U.S. Military Academy Combating Terrorism Center, December 2010.
[13] Peter Bergen and Bruce Hoffman, "Assessing the Terrorist Threat," *A Report of the Bipartisan Policy Center's National Security Preparedness Group*, September, 2010.
[14] Rohan Gunaratna and Aviv Oreg, "Al Qaeda's Organizational Structure and its Evolution," *Studies in Conflict & Terrorism*, vol. 33, no. 12 (December 2010).
[15] Prepared by Kenneth Katzman, Specialist in Middle Eastern Affairs.
[16] The Muslim Brotherhood was founded in 1928 in Egypt, and it has since spawned numerous Islamist movements throughout the region, some as branches of the Brotherhood, others with new names. For example, the Palestinian Islamist group Hamas traces its roots to the Palestinian branch of the Muslim Brotherhood. In 1966, Sayyid Qutb was tried and executed for treason for his opposition to the government of Egyptian President Gamal Abd al Nasser.
[17] Rohan Gunaratna, *Inside Al Qaeda*. Columbia University Press, 2002; Wright, Lawrance. *The Looming Tower: Al Qaeda and the Road to 9/11*. New York, Knopf, 2006. pp. 60-144.
[18] The September 11 Commission report says that U.S. officials obtained information in 2000 indicating that bin Laden received $1 million per year from his family from 1970 (two years after his father's death) until 1994, when his citizenship was revoked by the Saudi government. *Final Report of the National Commission on Terrorist Attacks Upon the United States*. July 22, 2004. p. 170.
[19] Gunaratna, p. 21.
[20] Author conversations with officials in the public affairs office of the Central Intelligence Agency. 1993.
[21] Report of the 9/11 Commission. p. 67.
[22] On December 21, 2004, the Treasury Department designated Faqih as a provider of material support to Al Qaeda and Bin Laden, under Executive Order 13324.
[23] Prepared by Kenneth Katzman, Specialist in Middle Eastern Affairs.
[24] For text of the summary of the review, see http://www.google.com/search?hl=en&source=hp&q=overview+of+the+afghanistan+and+pakistan+annual+review&aq=0&aqi=g1&aql=&oq=overview+of+the+afgha& gs_rfai=.
[25] Text of the Panetta interview with ABC News is at http://abcnews.go.com/print?id=11025299.
[26] Dreazen, Yochi. "Al Qaida Returning to Afghanistan for New Attacks." Nationaljournal.com. October 18, 2010.
[27] See for example, Berntsen, Gary. Jawbreaker, New York: Crown Publishers, 2005.
[28] Starr, Barbara: "NATO Official: Bin Laden, Deputy Hiding in Northwest Pakistan." CNN, October 18, 2010. http://articles.cnn.com/2010-10-18/world/afghanistan.bin.laden_1_tribal-areas-al-qaeda-leadership-chitral?_s=PM:WORLD.
[29] Gall, Carlotta and Ismail Khan. "U.S. Drone Attack Missed Zawahiri by Hours." New York Times, November 10, 2006.
[30] Prepared by Alan Kronstadt, Specialist in South Asian Affairs.
[31] During a late 2009 visit to Islamabad, U.S. Joint Chiefs Chairman Adm. Mike Mullen asserted that over the past 12- 24 months Pakistan-based terrorist groups including Al Qaeda, the Afghan Taliban, the Pakistani Taliban, Lashkar-eTaiba, and Jaish-e-Mohammed were "working much more closely together." Michael Leiter , Director of the National Counterterrorism Center, more recently called this "diversification" of the threat "most difficult for the counterterrorism community" (see the Pentagon's December 16, 2009, transcript at http://www.jcs.mil/speech.aspx? ID=1298; Aspen Security Forum 2010,

"Counterrorism Strategy with the Hon. Michael E Leiter, Director, National Counterterrorism Center," June 30, 2010).

[32] "NATO Official: Bin Laden, Deputy Hiding in Northwest Pakistan," CNN.com (online), October 18, 2010; "'Heart' of Al Qaeda in Afghan-Pakistani Border Area: Gates," Agence France Presse, November 9, 2010.

[33] See, for example, "Qaeda's Zawahri Urges Pakistanis to Join Jihad," Reuters, July 15, 2009. More recently, Al Qaeda figures criticized the Islamabad government for its allegedly corrupt and inept response to the major flood disaster ("Bin Laden Criticizes Pakistani Relief Mission," Reuters, October 1, 2010).

[34] "New Estimate of Strength of Al Qaeda is Offered," *New York Times*, July 1, 2010.

[35] "Qaeda's Training Areas in Pakistan Notorious," *New York Daily News*, September 21, 2009; "Terror Training Camps Smaller, Harder to Target," Associated Press, November 9, 2009; Barbara Sude, "Al Qaeda Central," New American Foundation Counterterrorism Strategy Initiative Policy Paper, February 2010; "Pakistan Retains Allure for Terror Trainees," *Wall Street Journal*, May 5, 2010.

[36] "Pakistan Al Qaeda Aids Yemen Plots," *Wall Street Journal*, November 5, 2010.

[37] See http://www.dni.gov/press_releases/20070717_release.pdf.

[38] See http://www.whitehouse.gov/assets/documents/afghanistan_pakistan_white_ paper _final.pdf.

[39] See the State Department report at http://www.state.gov/s/ct/rls/crt/2009/index.htm.

[40] Don Rassler, "Al-Qa'ida's Pakistan Strategy," CTC Sentinel, June 2009.

[41] Ibid.

[42] See the State Department's October 30, 2009, transcript at http://www.state.gov/secretary/rm/2009a/10/131103.htm.

[43] The CIA Director repeatedly has asserted that increased Pakistani government coordination and what he called "the most aggressive operation that CIA has been involved in in our history" has driven Al Qaeda leaders into deeper hiding and disrupted their ability to operate ("CIA Director Says Attacks Have Hobbled Al Qaeda," Washington Post, March 18, 2010; "Stepped-Up U.S. Operations in Pakistan Taking Serious Toll on Al Qaeda, CIA Chief Says," Los Angeles Times, October 19, 2010).

[44] See data at the New American Foundation's "The Year of the Drone" at http://counterterrorism.newamerica.net/ drones. Since 2004, drone strikes reportedly have killed at least 15 senior and 15 mid-level Al Qaeda leaders. At least 80 members of the terrorist group were killed in drone strikes in 2010 ("Drones Take Toll on Al Qaeda Leaders," *USA Today*, June 3, 2010; "Inside Al Qaeda," *Newsweek*, September 13, 2010).

[45] "Spy Agencies Infiltrate Al Qaeda," Associated Press, November 5, 2010.

[46] The TTP was designated as a Foreign Terrorist Organization and Specially Designated Terrorist Organization under U.S. law in September 2010. A senior Obama Administration counterterrorism official describes the group as having a "symbiotic relationship" with Al Qaeda, offering safe havens in the FATA in return for "ideological guidance" and "force multiplier" assistance (see the September 1, 2010, comments of Ambassador-at-Large for Counterterrorism Daniel Benjamin at http://www.state.gov/s/ct/rls/rm/2010/146597.htm).

[47] Originally from Pakistani Kashmir, Kashmiri is identified as a rising Al Qaeda figure—the most senior non-Arab in the organization—with the experience, connections, and determination to make him a highly dangerous operative. In August 2010, the U.S. Treasury Department designated HuJI as a Foreign Terrorist Organization under U.S. law and named Kashmiri as a Specially Designated Global Terrorist. Today he is believed to be plotting *fedayeen* (suicide commando) attacks in western Europe and perhaps the United States

similar to that in Mumbai, India, in late 2008 that left 165 people dead. Kashmiri is a veteran of both the 1980s insurgency against the Soviet Army in Afghanistan and of the 1990s insurgency against the Indian Army in Kashmir. He has been linked to an effort to assassinate then-Pakistani leader Pervez Musharraf in 2003 and may have abetted the 2008 Mumbai attack ("Lashkar-e-Taiba Cadres Sucked Into Al Qaeda Orbit," Reuters, November 7, 2010; Treasury Department's August 6, 2010, notification at http://www.treas.gov/press/releases/tg818.htm; "The New Bin Laden," *Newsweek*, November 1, 2010; "Ilyas Kashmiri: Most Dangerous Man on Earth?," CNN.com (online), November 10, 2010).

[48] "Key Osama Aide Among 9 Terrorists Held in Karachi," *Daily Times* (Lahore), February 9, 2010; "Qaeda Operative the leadership of Saudi Arabia that much more needed to be done to protect vital installations of all kinds." Jim Landers, "Saudi Arabia Works to Protect Oil Fields from Terrorism," *Dallas Morning News*, December 5, 2007. In late April 2007, Saudi authorities arrested 170 terrorism suspects, citing charges of planning to target critical oil facilities in the Eastern Province. Dan Murphy, "New Saudi Tack on Al Qaeda," *Christian Science Monitor*, April 30, 2007.

[48] "Key Osama Aide Among 9 Terrorists Held in Karachi," Daily Times (Lahore), February 9, 2010; "Qaeda Operative Arrested in Pakistan," New York Times, March 8, 2010; Ali Chishti, "Terror Report Card: Pakistan" (op-ed), Daily Times (Lahore), November 14, 2010.

[49] "In Military Campaign, Pakistan Finds Hint of 9/11," New York Times, October 30, 2009; Paul Cruickshank, "The Militant Pipeline," New American Foundation Counterterrorism Strategy Initiative Policy Paper, February 2010.

[50] "Al Qaeda Could Provoke New India-Pakistan War: Gates," Agence France Presse, January 20, 2010.

[51] See the survey results at http://pewglobal.org/files/pdf/Pew-Global-Attitudes-2010-Pakistan-Report.pdf).

[52] Prepared by Jeremy M. Sharp, Specialist in Middle Eastern Affairs, and Christopher M. Blanchard, Analyst in Middle Eastern Affairs. For more information on Al Qaeda in the Arabian Peninsula, see CRS Report RL34170, Yemen: Background and U.S. Relations, by Jeremy M. Sharp, and CRS Report RL33533, Saudi Arabia: Background and U.S. Relations, by Christopher M. Blanchard.

[53] See OSC Feature FEA20090124809516, "Video Shows Saudi, Yemeni Al-Qa'ida Leaders Announcing Merger," January 24, 2009; and, OSC Report GMP20090128666004, "Al-Qa'ida Amir in Arabian Peninsula Urges Targeting 'Crusader' Interests," Al-Jazirah.net (Doha) January 26, 2009.

[54] Saudi counterterrorism officials appear confident that they have killed or captured most of the leaders and operatives that made up the original AQAP organization. King Abdullah echoed this sentiment in June 2006, when he stated that AQAP had been "defeated." "Saudi King Says Al Qaeda Militants Defeated," Reuters, June 7, 2006.

[55] The attack in February 2006 on the oil processing facility at Abqaiq was in some ways the most serious of Al Qaeda's attacks inside the kingdom. Accounts suggest that the attack came dangerously close to disrupting operations at one of the world's most critical oil facilities. Then-U.S. Ambassador James Oberwetter has stated that, "The Saudis fortunately deterred damage to the Abqaiq facilities, but al-Qaeda penetrated the plant site. This assault was evidence to the leadership of Saudi Arabia that much more needed to be done to protect vital installations of all kinds." Jim Landers, "Saudi Arabia Works to Protect Oil Fields from Terrorism," Dallas Morning News, December 5, 2007. In late April 2007, Saudi

authorities arrested 170 terrorism suspects, citing charges of planning to target critical oil facilities in the Eastern Province. Dan Murphy, "New Saudi Tack on Al Qaeda," *Christian Science Monitor*, April 30, 2007.

[56] The Prince counts four Al Qaeda attempts on his life and emphasizes the personal sacrifices made by Saudi security officers and their families in meetings with U.S. officials. OSC Document GMP20100816614007, "Saudi Paper Reveals Fourth Attempt To Assassinate Deputy Interior Prince Muhammad," *Ukaz*, August 16, 2010.

[57] Saudi national Sa'id al Shihri delivered an audio message entitled ""Together to Overthrow Al Sa'ud," posted online on August 9, 2010. Transcript in OSC Document GMP20100810535004.

[58] In November 2010, AQAP carried out a suicide bomb attack against a religious procession of Shiite rebels observing the festival of Al Ghadeer, a holiday which commemorates the appointment of Ali ibn Abi Talib by the prophet Muhammad as his immediate successor. The bombing killed 23 people.

[59] The population of Yemen is almost entirely Muslim, divided between Zaydis, found in much of the north (and a majority in the northwest), and Shafi'is, found mainly in the south and east. Zaydis belong to a branch of Shi'a Islam, while Shafi'is follow one of several Sunni Muslim legal schools. Yemen's Zaydis take their name from their fifth Imam, Zayd ibn Ali. They are doctrinally distinct from the Twelvers, the dominant branch of Shi'a Islam in Iran and Lebanon. Twelver Shiites believe that the 12th Imam, Muhammad al Mahdi, has been hidden by Allah and will reappear on Earth as the savior of mankind.

[60] Several of AQAP's Yemeni leaders were among those freed in a now infamous jailbreak in 2006, in which 23 convicted terrorists escaped from a supposedly high-security prison in the capital of Sana'a.

[61] "Al-Qaeda's Yemen affiliate widens search for recruits and targets," *Washington Post*, November 30, 2010.

[62] It is worth noting that until the failed bomb attack against Northwest Airlines Flight 253 on Christmas Day 2009, most non-governmental observers believed that AQAP's influence and ability to threaten U.S. and Western interests from Yemen remained limited. In assessing the AQAP threat to the American homeland, a May 2010 Senate Intelligence Committee report concluded that U.S. intelligence agencies previously saw AQAP (before the December 25, 2009, attempted airline bombing) as a threat to American targets in Yemen, not to the United States itself. See, U.S. Congress, Senate Select Committee on Intelligence, ATTEMPTED TERRORIST ATTACK ON NORTHWEST AIRLINES FLIGHT 253, 111th Cong., 2nd sess., May 24, 2010, 111-199 (Washington: GPO, 2010).

[63] Twenty-nine-year-old Saudi citizen Ibrahim Hassan al Asiri is believed to have created the explosive devices used in last year's Christmas Day attempted bombing of Northwest Airlines Flight 253, in a 2009 attack against Saudi Arabia's intelligence chief Mohammed bin Nayef, and the October 2010 air cargo packages destined for Jewish sites in Chicago.

[64] "FACTBOX: Qaeda Unveils "Strategy of a Thousands Cuts",," *Reuters*, November 21, 2010.

[65] It is unclear whether the information was derived from Saudi national and former Guantanamo Bay detainee Jabir al Fayfi, who turned himself in to authorities in Yemen in October 2010. A man appeared on Saudi state television in late December 2010 and early January 2011 under that name to offer an account of his time as an Al Qaeda operative and his surrender to Yemeni and Saudi authorities. See OSC Report GMP20101223877001, "Saudi TV Hosts Former Wanted Person Al-Fayfi To Speak About Personal Experience," December 21, 2010.

[66] "Yemen Covert Role Pushed ," *Wall Street Journal*, November 1, 2010.

[67] "U.S. deploying drones in Yemen to hunt for Al-Qaeda, has yet to fire missiles," *Washington Post*, November 7, 2010.

[68] "White House to Yemen: Share more now," *Washington Post*, November 8, 2010.

[69] "More U.S. Funds Sought for Yemen's Forces," *Wall Street Journal*, September 3, 2010.

[70] "Is Yemen the Next Afghanistan?," *New York Times*, July 6, 2010.

[71] "Yemen Walks Fine Line in Aiding U.S," *Washington Post*, January 5, 2010.

[72] This section was prepared by Carol Migdalovitz, former Specialist in Middle Eastern Affairs, Nicolas Cook, Specialist in African Affairs, and Lauren Ploch, Analyst in African Affairs. For additional background and information on AQIM in North Africa, please contact Alexis Arieff, Analyst in African Affairs. See CRS Report RS21532, *Algeria: Current Issues*; CRS Report RS21579, *Morocco: Current Issues*; and CRS Report RS21666, *Tunisia: Recent Developments and Policy Issues*, all by Carol Migdalovitz, for additional background and information.

[73] Paul Taylor, "PM Says France "at War" with Al Qaeda Over Hostage," Reuters, July, 2010; Voice of America, "French Police: Al-Qaida Could Hit France," September 22, 2010; Erika Solomon, "Bin Laden Blames French "Injustice" for Abductions-TV," Reuters, October 27, 2010, among other sources.

[74] GIA remains on the State Department's list of Foreign Terrorist Organizations (FTO's), although its heyday ended in 2001and it has not perpetrated an attack since 2006.

[75] Michael Jonson and Christian Nils Larson, "Illegal Tender: Funding Al-Qaeda in the Islamic Maghrib," *Janes Intelligence Review*, October 2008.

[76] U.S. Department of State, *Country Reports on Terrorism*, 2008, April 30, 2009; and Lamine Chikhi, "Algerian Insurgents Seeking Out New Targets," August 17, 2009.

[77] Some attributed the second ambush to the Protectors of Salafi Call, which reportedly had split from the GSPC and, therefore, is not considered AQIM.[77] Others attributed the attack to a regional command of AQIM and still others suggested that AQIM is encroaching on the Protectors' territory. BBC Monitoring Middle East, "Five Regions Reportedly Designated for 'Terrorist Deployment' in Algeria," *El Khabar* website, August 5, 2009; and, BBC Monitoring Newsfile, "Retreating of the Salafi Call Protectors," *Echourouk el Youmi* website, August 17, 2009.

[78] See, e.g., Christian Lowe and Lamine Chikhi, "Ambush in Sahara Kills 11 Algerian Police - Report," June 30, 2010.

[79] Emily Andrews, "Big Bang Scientist Admits Plotting Al Qaeda Atrocity," *Daily Mail*, October 12, 2009.

[80] U.S. Department of State, "Travel Warning: Mauritania," December 2, 2009.

[81] These and other hostage releases have reportedly been made possible by ransom payments, but such payments are sensitive and have never been confirmed by governments involved in negotiations. There has also been controversy over AQIM prisoner releases under release deals. Mauritania and Algeria have criticized Mali for releasing prisoners in response to AQIM demands in order to secure kidnapped hostage releases. However, in August 2010 Mauritania extradited to Mali an AQIM prisoner who was then released in exchange for two kidnapped Spanish aid workers. The deal also reportedly involved a ransom payment.

[82] The group led by Djouadi and a key commander, Abid Hammadou (commonly known as Abu Zeid), is linked closely to AQIM's Algerian leadership. The MBM group operates semi-autonomously. MBM is a Mali-based former GIA and GSPC member who reportedly split from the GSPC after opposing Droukdel's accession to the GSPC leadership. See U.S. Treasury, "Treasury Targets Al Qaida-Affiliated Terror Group in Algeria," July 17, 2008; Geoffrey York, "The Shadowy Negotiator Who Freed Fowler and Guay," *Globe and Mail*,

October 17, 2009;, Reuters, "Mali Arrests Four Al Qaeda Members Near Algeria," May 1, 2009; and Reuters, "The Main Players in Al Qaeda's Saharan Operations," August 12, 2010, *inter alia*.

[83] Andrew Black, "Mokhtar Belmokhtar: The Algerian Jihad's Southern Amir," *Terrorism Monitor*, (7:12), May, 2009; and U.N. Security Council (UNSC), Committee pursuant to resolution 1267 (1999), and other sources.

[84] State Department, FY2011 Congressional Budget Justification. TSCTP includes Algeria, Burkina Faso, Chad, Mali, Mauritania, Morocco, Niger, Nigeria, Senegal, and Tunisia. Libya has been invited to join. Countries nominated for TSCTP membership by a USG agency are consulted and must agree on the designation.

[85] For more information, see CRS Report RL34003, *Africa Command: U.S. Strategic Interests and the Role of the U.S. Military in Africa*, by Lauren Ploch.

[86] TSCTP and OEF-TS capacity building activities with Chad, Mauritania, and Niger were limited in FY2009 due to U.S. government restrictions. Sanctions on Mauritania, applied after the 2008 coup, were lifted in September 2009. Programming in Chad and Niger has been restricted due to both political concerns and human rights vetting issues.

[87] Prepared by Ted Dagne, Specialist in African Affairs.

[88] http://www.bbc.co.uk/news/10602791.

[89] The 2005 U.S. State Department Country Report on Terrorism described Al Ittihad Al Islami as "a Somali extremist group that was formed in the 1980s and reached its peak in the early 1990s, failed to obtain its objective of establishing a Salafist emirate in Somalia and steadily declined following the downfall of the Siad Barre regime in 1991 and Somalia's subsequent collapse into anarchy. AIAI was not internally cohesive, lacked central leadership, and suffered divisions between factions."

[90] For more on Al-Shabaab and other terror groups, see CRS Report RL 33911, *Somalia: Current Conditions and Prospects for Lasting Peace*, by Ted Dagne.

[91] Ted Dagne interviewed President Sheik Sharif Ahmad of Somalia and other senior officials, January 29 and February 1, 2010.

[92] For more information on U.S. counterterrorism programs in the region, see CRS Report R41473, *Countering Terrorism in East Africa: The U.S. Response*, by Lauren Ploch.

[93] Director of National Intelligence Dennis C. Blair, Annual Threat Assessment of the U.S. Intelligence Community for the Senate Select Committee on Intelligence, February 2, 2010.

[94] See "Young Somali Men Missing from Minneapolis," *International Herald Tribune*, November 27, 2008. In March 2009, an NCTC official expressed "concern... over the travel by some tens of Somali-American young men back to Somalia, some of whom have trained and fought with Al Shabaab." Testimony of Andrew Liepman, Deputy Director, Intelligence, National Counterterrorism Center before the Senate Homeland Security and Governmental Affairs Committee, March 11, 2009.

[95] Testimony of Andrew Liepman, op cit. "Let me stress we don't have a body of reporting that indicates U.S. persons who have traveled to Somalia are planning to execute attacks in the United States. We don't have that credible reporting. But we do worry that there is the potential that these individuals could be indoctrinated by al Qaeda while they're in Somalia and then returned to the United States with the intention to conduct attacks."

[96] Prepared by Bruce Vaughn, Specialist in Asian Affairs, ext. 7-3144. For more, see CRS Report RL34194, *Terrorism in Southeast Asia*, coordinated by Bruce Vaughn.

[97] "Indonesia Jails Driver Over Jakarta Hotel Bomb," *BBC News*, June 14, 2010.

[98] "Are Indonesian Terror Networks Regrouping?" *BBC News,* March 10, 2010. Sydney Jones, Remarks with Ernest Bower, Center for Strategic and International Studies, Washington, DC, 2010.
[99] Tom Allard, "Police Mount Terrorist Raids in Lead-up to Obama's Visit," *The Sydney Morning Herald,* May 14, 2010.
[100] Ashish Kumar Sen, ""Terrorists Planned to Kill President During Obama Visit; Mumbai-Style Strike was Goal," *The Washington Times,* May 18, 2010.
[101] Tom Allard, "Indonesia Terror Laws to Change," *The Age,* June 5, 2010. "SBY Hopes Terrorist Arrest Cripples Cell," *The Jakarta Post,* June 24, 2010.
[102] Sydney Jones, Remarks with Ernest Bower, Center for Strategic and International Studies, Washington, DC, 2010.
[103] "Bali Bomber Dulmatin Confirmed Dead," *BBC News,* March 10, 2010.
[104] Fatima Astuti, "Indonesia's National Counter Terrorism Agency," *International Centre for Political Violence and Terrorism,* October 2010.
[105] "Indonesia's National Counter Terrorism Agency," *Eurasia Review,* October 11, 2010.
[106] "Indonesia Seeks Renewed Anti-Terror Fight," *Sydney Morning Herald,* October 18, 2010.
[107] Salim Osman, "Joint Terror Op Sparks Debate in Indonesia," *The Straits Times,* October 12, 2010.
[108] "Military Vows to Crush Terrorist Network," The Jakareta Post, September 27, 2010.
[109] "Ba'asyir Linked to Medan Group," *Koran Tempo,* October 9, 2010.
[110] Prepared by Christopher M. Blanchard, Analyst in Middle Eastern Affairs.
[111] Vahid Brown, "Al Qa'ida Central and Local Affiliates," p. 69, in Assaf Moghadam and Brian Fishman (eds.), *Self-Inflicted Wounds: Debates and Divisions within Al Qaeda and its Periphery,* U.S. Military Academy Combating Terrorism Center, December 2010.
[112] Assaf Moghadam and Brian Fishman, "Debates and Divisions Within and Around Al Qa'ida," pp. 11-2, in Moghadam and Fishman, (eds.) *Self-Inflicted Wounds,* December 2010.
[113] In December 2010, the Pew Global Attitudes Project released the findings of a survey of Muslims in Turkey, Nigeria, Pakistan, Jordan, Egypt, Indonesia and Lebanon that found, with the exception of the surveyed group in Nigeria, "opinions of al Qaeda and its leader, Osama bin Laden, are consistently negative." The survey also suggests that support for suicide bombing and confidence in Osama bin Laden among Muslims surveyed has declined steeply since 2003. Pew Research Center "Muslim Publics Divided on Hamas and Hezbollah: Most Embrace a Role for Islam in Politics," December 2, 2010.
[114] Some analysts believe that violent Islamist appeals that fit a model of so-called "classical jihad" by calling for an armed response to "the presence of foreigners on Muslim territory" have more popular resonance and are viewed as more religiously legitimate than Al Qaeda's appeals for "global jihad," which seek to mobilize Muslims in response to "a wider range of grievances, including perceived Western cultural imperialism and financial support for regimes [Al Qaeda figures] deem unacceptable." Fishman and Moghadam, "Do Jihadi and Islamist Divisions Matter? Implications for Policy and Strategy," p. 230, in Moghadam and Fishman, (eds.) *Self-Inflicted Wounds,* December 2010.
[115] Assaf Moghadam and Brian Fishman, "Debates and Divisions Within and Around Al Qa'ida," pp. 8, in Moghadam and Fishman, (eds.) *Self-Inflicted Wounds,* December 2010.

In: The Death of Osama bin Laden ... ISBN: 978-1-61470-479-9
Editor: Raymond V. Donahue © 2011 Nova Science Publishers, Inc.

Chapter 3

U.S. SPECIAL OPERATIONS FORCES (SOF): BACKGROUND AND ISSUES FOR CONGRESS[*]

Andrew Feickert and Thomas K. Livingston

SUMMARY

Special Operations Forces (SOF) play a significant role in U.S. military operations, and the Administration has given U.S. SOF greater responsibility for planning and conducting worldwide counterterrorism operations. U.S. Special Operations Command (USSOCOM) has close to 60,000 active duty, National Guard, and reserve personnel from all four services and Department of Defense (DOD) civilians assigned to its headquarters, its four components, and one sub-unified command. The 2010 Quadrennial Defense Review (QDR) directs increases in SOF force structure, particularly in terms of increasing enabling units and rotary and fixed-wing SOF aviation assets and units. USSOCOM Commander, Admiral Eric T. Olson, in commenting on the current state of the forces under his command, noted that since September 11, 2001, USSOCOM manpower has nearly doubled, the budget nearly tripled, and overseas deployments have quadrupled; because of this high level of demand, the admiral added, SOF is beginning to show some "fraying around the edges" and one potential way to combat this is by finding ways to get

---

[*] This is an edited, reformatted and augmented version of a Congressional Research Service publication, CRS Report for Congress RS21048, from www.crs.gov, dated March 28, 2011.

SOF "more time at home." Admiral Olson also noted the effectiveness of Section 1208 authority, which provides funds for SOF to train and equip regular and irregular indigenous forces to conduct counterterrorism operations.

Vice Admiral William McRaven, the current commander of the Joint Special operations Command (JSOC) has been recommended by the Secretary of Defense for nomination to replace Admiral Olson, who is retiring this year, as USSOCOM Commander. USSOCOM's FY2012 Budget Request is $10.5 billion—with $7.2 billion in the baseline budget and $3.3 billion in the Overseas Contingency Operations (OCO) budget, representing an increase of seven percent over the FY2011 Budget Request of $9.8 billion.

There are potential issues for congressional consideration. U.S. SOF in Iraq are in the process of transitioning counterterror operations in Iraq to Iraqi SOF and lessons learned could assist Congress in its oversight role. Another issue is that on January 6, 2011, Secretary of Defense Gates and Chairman of the Joint Chiefs of Staff Admiral Mike Mullen announced starting in FY2015, the Army would decrease its permanently authorized endstrength by 27,000 soldiers and that the Marines would lose anywhere between 15,000 to 20,000 Marines. Because USSOCOM draws their operators and support troops from the Services—primarily from the non-commissioned officer (NCO) and junior officer ranks—USSOCOM will have a smaller force pool to draw its members from. In addition, because the Services will have fewer troops, they might not be as receptive to USSOCOM recruitment efforts in order to keep high-quality NCOs and junior officers in their conventional units. Another implication is that these force reductions might also have an impact on the creation and sustainment of Army and Marine Corps "enabling" units that USSOCOM is seeking to support operations.

Another potential issue involves initiatives to get more "time at home" for SOF troops to help reduce stress on service members and their families. One of the major factors cited by USSOCOM leadership regarding "time away from family" is that SOF does not either have access to or the appropriate types of training facilities near their home stations, thereby necessitating travel away from their bases and families to conduct pre-deployment training. While the creation of additional local SOF training facilities might seem to be an obvious solution to this problem, the availability of land for military use as well as existing environmental regulations could make it difficult for USSOCOM to create new training facilities or modify existing facilities to suit SOF training requirements.

BACKGROUND

Overview

Special Operations Forces (SOF) are elite military units with special training and equipment that can infiltrate into hostile territory through land, sea, or air to conduct a variety of operations, many of them classified. SOF personnel undergo rigorous selection and lengthy specialized training. The U.S. Special Operations Command (USSOCOM) oversees the training, doctrine, and equipping of all U.S. SOF units.

Command Structures and Components

In 1986 Congress, concerned about the status of SOF within overall U.S. defense planning, passed measures (P.L. 99-661) to strengthen special operations' position within the defense community. These actions included the establishment of USSOCOM as a new unified command. USSOCOM is headquartered at MacDill Air Force Base in Tampa, FL. The Commander of USSOCOM is a four-star officer who may be from any military service. The current commander is Navy Admiral Eric T. Olson, who reports directly to the Secretary of Defense, although an Assistant Secretary of Defense for Special Operations and Low Intensity Conflict and Interdependent Capabilities (ASD/SOLIC&IC) provides immediate civilian oversight over many USSOCOM activities.

USSOCOM has about 58,000 active duty, National Guard, and reserve personnel from all four services and Department of Defense (DOD) civilians assigned to its headquarters, its four components, and one sub-unified command.[1] USSOCOM's components are the U.S. Army Special Operations Command (USASOC); the Naval Special Warfare Command (NAVSPECWARCOM); the Air Force Special Operations Command (AFSOC); and the Marine Corps Special Operations Command (MARSOC). The Joint Special Operations Command (JSOC) is a USSOCOM sub-unified command.

Expanded USSOCOM Responsibilities

In addition to its Title 10 authorities and responsibilities, USSOCOM has been given additional responsibilities. In the 2004 Unified Command Plan, USSOCOM was given the responsibility for synchronizing DOD plans against global terrorist networks and, as directed, conducting global operations against those networks.[2] In this regard, USSOCOM "receives, reviews, coordinates and prioritizes all DOD plans that support the global campaign against terror, and then makes recommendations to the Joint Staff regarding force and resource allocations to meet global requirements."[3] In October 2008, USSOCOM was designated as the DOD proponent for Security Force Assistance (SFA).[4] In this role, USSOCOM will perform a synchronizing function in global training and assistance planning similar to the previously described role of planning against terrorist networks. In addition, USSOCOM is now DOD's lead for countering threat financing, working with the U.S. Treasury and Justice Departments on means to identify and disrupt terrorist financing efforts.

Army Special Operations Forces

U.S. Army SOF (ARSOF) includes approximately 28,500 soldiers from the Active Army, National Guard, and Army Reserve who are organized into Special Forces, Ranger, and special operations aviation units, along with civil affairs units, psychological operations units, and special operations support units. ARSOF Headquarters and other resources, such as the John F. Kennedy Special Warfare Center and School, are located at Fort Bragg, NC. Five active Special Forces (SF) Groups (Airborne),[5] consisting of about 1,400 soldiers each, are stationed at Fort Bragg and at Fort Lewis, WA, Fort Campbell, KY, Fort Carson, CO, and Eglin Air Force Base, FL. Special Forces soldiers—also known as the Green Berets—are trained in various skills, including foreign languages, that allow teams to operate independently throughout the world. In December 2005, the 528th Sustainment Brigade (Special Operations) (Airborne) was activated at Ft. Bragg, NC, to provide combat service support and medical support to Army special operations forces.[6]

In FY2008, the U.S. Army Special Operations Command (USASOC) began to increase the total number of Army Special Forces battalions from 15 to 20, with one battalion being allocated to each active Special Forces Group. In August 2008, the Army stood up the first of these new battalions—the 4th

Battalion, 5th Special Forces Groups (Airborne)—at Fort Campbell, KY.[7] The Army expects that the last of these new Special Forces battalions will be operational by FY2013.[8] Two Army National Guard Special Forces groups are headquartered in Utah and Alabama. An elite airborne light infantry unit specializing in direct action operations[9], the 75th Ranger Regiment, is headquartered at Fort Benning, GA, and consists of three battalions. Army special operations aviation units, including the 160th Special Operations Aviation Regiment (Airborne), headquartered at Fort Campbell, KY, feature pilots trained to fly the most sophisticated Army rotary-wing aircraft in the harshest environments, day or night, and in adverse weather.

Some of the most frequently deployed SOF assets are civil affairs (CA) units, which provide experts in every area of civil government to help administer civilian affairs in operational theaters. The 95th Civil Affairs Brigade (Airborne) is the only active CA unit; all other CA units reside in the Reserves and are affiliated with conventional Army units. Military Information Support Operations units disseminate information to large foreign audiences through mass media. The active duty 4th Military Information Support Group (MISO), (Airborne) is stationed at Fort Bragg, and two Army Reserve MISO groups work with conventional Army units.

Air Force Special Operations Forces[10]

The Air Force Special Operations Command (AFSOC) is one of the Air Force's 10 major commands with over 12,000 active duty personnel and over 16,000 personnel when civilians, Guard and Reserve personnel and units are included. While administrative control of AFSOC is overseen by the Chief of Staff of the Air Force (CSAF), operational control is managed by the USSOCOM Commander. AFSOC units operate out of four major continental Unite States (CONUS) locations and two overseas locations. The headquarters for AFSOC, the first Special Operations Wing (1st SOW), and the 720th Special Tactics Group are located at Hurlburt Field, FL. The 27th SOW is at Cannon AFB, NM. The 352nd and 353rd Special Operations Groups provide forward presence in Europe (RAF Mildenhall, England) and in the Pacific (Kadena Air Base, Japan) respectively. The Air National Guard's 193rd SOW at Harrisburg, PA, and the Air Force Reserve Command's 919th SOW at Duke Field, FL, complete AFSOC's major units. A training center, the U.S. Air Force Special Operations School and Training Center (AFSOTC), was recently established and is located at Hurlburt Field. AFSOC conducts the majority of its specialized flight training through an arrangement with Air Education and Training Command (AETC) via the 550th SOW at Kirtland AFB, NM. AFSOC's four active-duty flying units are composed of more than 100 fixed and rotary-wing aircraft.

In March 2009, Headquarters AFSOC declared initial operational capability (IOC)[11] for the CV-22.[12] USSOCOM plans for all 50 CV-22s to be delivered to AFSOC by 2015.[13] Since 2009, AFSOC has completed three overseas deployments, to Central America, Africa, and Iraq, and continues to be engaged currently in overseas contingency operations. Despite critical reviews of the aircraft, AFSOC considers the CV-22 "central to our future."[14] AFSOC operates a diverse fleet of modified aircraft. Of 12 major design series aircraft, 7 are variants of the C-130, the average age of some of which is over 40 years old and date from the Viet Nam era. Because of the age of the fleet, AFSOC considers recapitalization one of its top priorities.

AFSOC's Special Tactics experts include Combat Controllers, Pararescue Jumpers, Special Operations Weather Teams, and Tactical Air Control Party (TACPs). As a collective group, they are known as Special Tactics and have also been referred to as "Battlefield Airmen." Their basic role is to provide an interface between air and ground forces, and these airmen have very developed skill sets. Usually embedded with Army, Navy, or Marine SOF units, they provide control of air fire support, medical and rescue expertise, or weather support, depending on the mission requirements.

As directed in the 2010 QDR, AFSOC plans to increase aviation advisory manpower and resources resident in the 6th Special Operations Squadron (SOS). The 6th SOS's mission is to assess, train, and advise partner nation aviation units with the intent to raise their capability and capacity to interdict threats to their nation. The 6th SOS provides aviation expertise to U.S. foreign internal defense (FID) missions.

Naval Special Operations Forces[15]

The Naval Special Warfare Command (NSWC) consists of about 8,800 military and civilian personnel and is located in Coronado, CA. NSWC is organized around 10 SEAL Teams, two SEAL Delivery Vehicle (SDV) Teams, and three Special Boat Teams. SEAL Teams consist of six SEAL platoons each, consisting of two officers and 16 enlisted personnel. The major operational components of NSWC include Naval Special Warfare Groups One, Three, and Eleven, stationed in Coronado, CA, and Naval Special

Warfare Groups Two and Four and the Naval Special Warfare Development Group in Little Creek, VA. These components deploy SEAL Teams, SEAL Delivery Vehicle Teams, and Special Boat Teams worldwide to meet the training, exercise, contingency and wartime requirements of theater commanders. SEALs are considered the best-trained combat swimmers in the world, and can be deployed covertly from submarines or from sea and land-based aircraft.

Marine Special Operations Command (MARSOC)[16]

On November 1, 2005, DOD announced the creation of the Marine Special Operations Command (MARSOC) as a component of USSOCOM. MARSOC consists of three subordinate units—the Marine Special Operations Regiment, which includes 1st, 2nd, and 3rd Marine Special Operations Battalions; the Marine Special Operations Support Group; the Marine Special Operations Intelligence Battalion; and the Marine Special Operations School. MARSOC Headquarters, the 2nd and 3rd Marine Special Operations Battalions, the Marine Special Operations School, and the Marine Special Operations Support Group and the Marine Special Operations Intelligence Battalion are stationed at Camp Lejeune, NC. The 1st Marine Special Operations Battalion is stationed at Camp Pendleton, CA. MARSOC forces have been deployed worldwide to conduct a full range of special operations activities. By 2014, MARSOC is planned to have about 3,000 marines, sailors, and civilians.

Marine Corps Force Structure Review[17]

In the fall of 2010, the Marines Corps conducted a force structure review that focused on the post Operation Enduring Freedom [Afghanistan] security environment. This review had a number of recommendations for Marine forces, including MARSOC. The review called for strengthening MARSOC by more than 1,000 Marines including a 44% increase in critical combat support and service support Marines. It is currently not known how these proposed increases will translate into additional capabilities and new force structure and how much these proposed additions will cost.

Joint Special Operations Command (JSOC)

According to DOD, the JSOC is "a joint headquarters designed to study special operations requirements and techniques; ensure interoperability and equipment standardization; plan and conduct joint special operations exercises and training; and develop joint special operations tactics."[18] While not officially acknowledged by DOD or USSOCOM, JSOC, which is headquartered at Pope Air Force Base, NC, is widely believed to command and control what are described as the military's special missions units—the Army's Delta Force, the Navy's SEAL Team Six, the 75th Ranger Regiment, the 160th Special Operations Aviation Regiment and the Air Force's 24th Special Tactics Squadron.[19] JSOC's primary mission is believed to be identifying and destroying terrorists and terror cells worldwide.

A recent news release by the U.S. Army Special Operations Command (USASOC) News Service which names Vice Admiral William McRaven as Admiral Olson's successor seemingly adds credibility to press reports about JSOC's alleged counterterrorism mission. The USASOC press release notes: "McRaven, a former commander of SEAL Team 3 and Special Operations Command Europe, is the commander of the Joint Special Operations Command. As such, he has led the command as it "ruthlessly and effectively [took] the fight to America's most dangerous and vicious enemies," Gates said."[20]

NATO Special Operations Headquarters[21]

In May 2010, NATO established the NATO Special Operations Headquarters (NSHQ), which is commanded by U.S. Air Force Lieutenant General Frank Kisner, who had previously commanded U.S. Special Operations Command—Europe (SOCEUR). The NSHQ is envisioned to serve as the core of a combined joint force special operations component command, which would be the proponent for planning, training, doctrine, equipping, and evaluating NATO special operations forces from 22 countries. The NSHQ is located with the Supreme Headquarters Allied Powers Europe (SHAPE) in Mons, Belgium, and will consist of about 150 NATO personnel.

CURRENT ORGANIZATIONAL AND BUDGETARY ISSUES

Pending Change in USSOCOM Leadership[22]

Vice Admiral William McRaven, the current commander of JSOC, has been recommended for nomination to replace Admiral Olson (who is retiring this year) as USSOCOM Commander. From the U.S. Army Special Operations Command News Service:

> Defense Secretary Robert M. Gates is recommending that President Barack Obama nominate Vice Adm. William McRaven for a fourth star and to the position of commander, U.S. Special Operations Command. ... Gates made the recommendations during a Pentagon press briefing March 1. If confirmed by the Senate, McRaven would succeed Navy Adm. Eric Olson, who has headed the command since 2008.

2010 Quadrennial Defense Review (QDR) Report SOF-Related Directives[23]

The 2010 QDR contains a number of SOF-related directives pertaining to personnel, organizations, and equipment. These include the following:

- To increase key enabling assets[24] for special operations forces.
- To maintain approximately 660 special operations teams;[25] 3 Ranger battalions; and 165 tilt-rotor/fixed-wing mobility and fire support primary mission aircraft.
- The Army and USSOCOM will add a company of upgraded cargo helicopters (MH-47G) to the Army's 160th Special Operations Aviation Regiment.
- The Navy will dedicate two helicopter squadrons for direct support to naval special warfare units.
- To increase civil affairs capacity organic to USSOCOM.
- Starting in FY2012, purchase light, fixed-wing aircraft to enable the Air Force's 6th Special Operations squadron to engage partner nations for whose air forces such aircraft might be appropriate, as well as acquiring two non-U.S. helicopters to support these efforts.

The significance of these directives are that they serve as definitive goals for USSOCOM growth and systems acquisition as well as directing how the Services will support USSOCOM.

2012 USSOCOM Defense Authorization Request and Posture Hearings[26]

In early March 2011, USSOCOM Commander Admiral Eric T. Olson testified to the Senate and House Armed Service Committees and, in addition to discussing budgetary requirements, also provided an update of the current state of U.S. SOF. Key points emphasized by Admiral Olson included the following:

- USSOCOM totals close to about 60,000 people with about 20,000 of whom are career members of SOF, meaning those who have been selected, trained, and qualified as SOF operators.
- Since September 11, 2001, USSOCOM manpower has nearly doubled, the budget nearly tripled, and overseas deployments have quadrupled. As an example, Admiral Olson noted that as 100,000 US troops came out of Iraq, fewer than 1,000 were from SOF and at the same time there was a requirement to move about 1,500 SOF to Afghanistan. As a result of this high demand for SOF, Admiral Olson stated that SOF is "fraying around the edges" and "showing signs of wear" but still remains a fundamentally strong and sound force.
- Admiral Olson further noted a slight increase in mid-career special operations troops with 8 to 10 years of service opting to leave the service.
- One of the key actions that USSOCOM is taking is to get SOF more "days at home" and predictability and part of that effort is trying to relieve SOF members of jobs or responsibilities that can be done by other individuals or units.
- One key problem that USOCOM faces that contributes to fewer "days at home" for SOF personnel is the lack of readily available, local ranges so that SOF can conduct pre-deployment training. Such a lack of local ranges means that SOF operators have to "travel to train" which further increases their time away from home.
- USSOCOM is also developing a force generation system that will better interface with the Service's force generation systems which is

U.S. Special Operations Forces (SOF)

- intended to provide better, more optimized force packages to the Geographic Combatant Commanders.
- Section 1208 authority (Section 1208 of P.L. 108-375, the FY2005 National Defense Authorization Act) provides authority and funds for U.S. SOF to train and equip regular and irregular indigenous forces to conduct counterterrorism operations. Section 1208 is considered a key tool in combating terrorism and is directly responsible for a number of highly successful counter-terror operations.
- Regarding equipment, USSOCOM is fielding the first of 72 planned MH-60M helicopters; is on the path to recapitalize the gunship fleet with AC-130J models; and the MC-130J program is on track to replace aging MC-130Es and MC130Ps. USSOCOM plans to award a competitive prototype contract later this year for the Combatant Craft-Medium (CCM) to replace the Special Warfare Rigid Hull Inflatable Boat (RHIB) and has also realigned funds from cancelled programs to fund the development of a family of Dry Submersibles that can be launched from surface ships or specialized submarines.

FY2012 USSOCOM Budget Request

USSOCOM's FY2012 Budget Request is $10.5 billion—with $7.2 billion in the baseline budget and $3.3 billion in the Overseas Contingency Operations (OCO) budget.[27] This represents an increase of seven percent over the FY2011 Budget Request of $9.8 billion. USSOCOM has long maintained that it represents about 2% of the Department of Defense budget and provides maximum operational impact for a limited investment. Another one of SOCOM's perceived benefits is that its components take proven, service-common equipment and modify it with SOF funding for special operations-unique capabilities.

POSSIBLE ISSUES FOR CONGRESS

Transition to Iraqi Special Operations Forces[28]

Reports suggest that after years of training by U.S. SOF, Iraqi SOF are now taking the lead in counterterrorism operations in Iraq. The almost 4,100 member Iraqi SOF are now planning and conducting their own missions with

U.S. SOF providing some intelligence assistance and post-mission advice. Some maintain that this represents a highly successful effort in building Iraq's indigenous counterterrorism capabilities from the ground up. Congress might examine the lessons learned from training and equipping Iraqi SOF for use in future oversight activities.

Potential Impact of Army and Marine Corps Downsizing[29]

On January 6, 2011, Secretary of Defense Gates and Chairman of the Joint Chiefs of Staff Admiral Mike Mullen announced that starting in FY2015, the Army would decrease its permanently authorized endstrength by 27,000 soldiers and that the Marines would lose anywhere between 15,000 to 20,000 Marines, depending on their force structure review. These downsizings have implications for USSOCOM. The first is that because USSOCOM draws their operators and support troops from the Services (primarily from the non-commissioned officer (NCO) and junior officer ranks) USSOCOM will have a smaller force pool to draw its members from. In addition, because the Service will have fewer troops, they might not be as receptive to USSOCOM recruitment efforts in order to keep high-quality NCOs and junior officers in their current units. Another implication is that these force reductions might also affect the creation and sustainment of Army and Marine Corps "enabling" units that USSOCOM is seeking to support operations. In this particular circumstance, Congress might decide to examine with the Services and USSOCOM how these downsizing efforts might affect the creation of enabling units.

Initiatives to Increase SOF "Days at Home"

Because USSOCOM growth is limited due to the high entrance standards for SOF candidates, while requirements to deploy SOF are likely to continue at the current rate, efforts to increase SOF "days at home" to decrease stress on SOF and their families will probably need to focus on times when SOF units are at their home stations. One of the major factors cited by USSOCOM leadership is that SOF units do not always have access to appropriate training facilities near their home stations, thereby necessitating travel away from their bases to conduct pre-deployment training. Given these circumstances, Congress might act to review USSOCOM proposals to improve the situation, whether by giving SOF priority access to existing training facilities, by modifying existing facilities to accommodate SOF training, or by building new SOF-dedicated training facilities closer to SOF bases. Factors that could limit efforts to improve SOF local training include the availability of land for military use, as well as existing environmental regulations that can preclude certain SOF-related training activities.

End Notes

[1] Information in this section is from "Fact Book: United States Special Operations Command," USSOCOM Public Affairs, February 2011, p. 7. DOD defines a sub-unified command as a command established by commanders of unified commands, when so authorized through the Chairman of the Joint Chiefs of Staff, to conduct operations on a continuing basis in accordance with the criteria set forth for unified commands. A subordinate unified command may be established on an area or functional basis. Commanders of subordinate unified commands have functions and responsibilities similar to those of the commanders of unified commands and exercise operational control of assigned commands and forces within the assigned joint operations area.

[2] "Fact Book: United States Special Operations Command," USSOCOM Public Affairs, February 2011, p. 4.

[3] Ibid.

[4] Information in this section is from testimony given by Admiral Eric T. Olson, Commander, U.S. SOCOM, to the House Terrorism, Unconventional Threats and Capabilities Subcommittee on the Fiscal Year 2010 National Defense Authorization Budget Request for the U.S. Special Operations Command, June 4, 2009.

[5] Airborne refers to "personnel, troops especially trained to effect, following transport by air, an assault debarkation, either by parachuting or touchdown." Joint Publication 1-02, Department of Defense Dictionary of Military and Associated Terms, 12 April 2001, (As Amended Through 31 July 2010).

[6] "Fact Book: United States Special Operations Command," USSOCOM Public Affairs, February 2011, p. 13.

[7] Sean D. Naylor, "Special Forces Expands," *Army Times,* August 11, 2008.

[8] Association of the United States Army, "U.S. Army Special Operations Forces: Integral to the Army and the Joint Force," *Torchbearer National Security Report,* March 2010, p. 3.

[9] Direct action operations are short-duration strikes and other small-scale offensive actions conducted as a special operation in hostile, denied, or politically sensitive environments, as well as employing specialized military capabilities to seize, destroy, capture, exploit, recover, or damage designated targets. Direct action differs from conventional offensive actions in the level of physical and political risk, operational techniques, and the degree of discriminate and precise use of force to achieve specific objectives.

[10] Information in this section is from Lt Gen Wurster's presentation to the Air Force Association, September 14 2010. http://www.afa.org/events/conference/2010/scripts/Wurster_9-14.pdf and "Fact Book: United States Special Operations Command," USSOCOM Public Affairs, February 2011.

[11] According to DOD IOC is attained when some units and/or organizations in the force structure scheduled to receive a system 1) have received it and 2) have the ability to employ and maintain it.

[12] The CV-22 is the special operations version of the V-22 Osprey tilt-rotor aircraft used by the Marine Corps.

[13] USSOCOM Acquisitions and Logistics office, http://www.socom.mil/soal/Pages/FixedWing.aspx.

[14] For further detailed reporting on the V-22 program, see CRS Report RL31384, *V-22 Osprey Tilt-Rotor Aircraft: Background and Issues for Congress*, by Jeremiah Gertler.

[15] Information in this section is from "Fact Book: United States Special Operations Command," USSOCOM Public Affairs, February 2011, pp. 20-21.

[16] Information in this section is from "Fact Book: United States Special Operations Command," USSOCOM Public Affairs, February 2011, p. 37.

[17] "Reshaping America's Expeditionary Force in Readiness: Report of the 2010 Marine Corps Force Structure Review Group," March 14, 2011.

[18] USSOCOM website http://www.socom.mil/components/components.htm, accessed March 19, 2008.

[19] Jennifer D. Kibbe, "The Rise of the Shadow Warriors," Foreign Affairs, Volume 83, Number 2, March/April 2004 and Sean D. Naylor, "JSOC to Become Three-Star Command," *Army Times*, February 13, 2006.

[20] U.S. Army Special Operations Command News Service, "Gates Nominates McRaven, Thurman for Senior Posts," Release Number: 110303-02, March 3, 2011, http://www.soc.mil/UNS/Releases/2011/March/110303-02.html.

[21] Information in this section is taken from Carlo Muñoz, "SOCEUR Chief Pegged: Air Force Two-Star to Head Up New NATO Special Ops Headquarters," *Inside the Air Force*, May 28, 2010 and NATO Fact Sheet, "NATO Special Operations Headquarters (NSHQ)," accessed from http://www.NATO.int on July 1, 2010.

[22] U.S. Army Special Operations Command News Service, "Gates Nominates McRaven, Thurman for Senior Posts," Release Number: 110303-02, March 3, 2011, http://www.soc.mil/ UNS/Releases/2011/March/110303-02.html.

[23] Information in this section is from Department of Defense, Quadrennial Defense Review Report, February 2010.

[24] Enabling assets are a variety of conventional military units that are assigned to support special operations forces.

[25] These teams include Army Special Forces Operational Detachment-Alpha (ODA) teams; Navy Sea, Air, and Land (SEAL) platoons; Marine special operations teams, Air Force special tactics teams; and operational aviation detachments.

[26] CQ Congressional Transcripts, Senate Armed Services Committee Holds Hearings on the Fiscal 2012 Defense Authorization Requests for the U.S. Special Operations Command and the U.S. Central Command, March 1, 2011 and Posture Statement of Admiral Eric T. Olson, USN, Commander, United States Special Operations Command Before the 112th Congress House Armed Services Committee March 3, 2011.

[27] Information in this section is from the United States Special Operations Command FY2012 Budget Estimates, February 2011 and Posture Statement of Admiral Eric T. Olson, USN, Commander, United States Special Operations Command Before the 112th Congress House Armed Services Committee March 3, 2011.

[28] Thomas Erdbrink, "In Iraq, U.S. Special Forces Gearing Up to Leave," *Washington Post,* March 24, 2011.
[29] Unless otherwise noted, information in this section is taken from U.S. Department of Defense News Transcript, "DOD News Briefing with Secretary Gates and Adm. Mike Mullen from the Pentagon" January 6, 2011.
http://www.defense.gov/transcripts/transcript.aspx?transcriptid=4747.

In: The Death of Osama bin Laden ...
Editor: Raymond V. Donahue

ISBN: 978-1-61470-479-9
© 2011 Nova Science Publishers, Inc.

Chapter 4

NAVY IRREGULAR WARFARE AND COUNTERTERRORISM OPERATIONS: BACKGROUND AND ISSUES FOR CONGRESS[*]

Ronald O'Rourke

SUMMARY

The Navy for several years has carried out a variety of irregular warfare (IW) and counterterrorism (CT) activities, and has taken some steps in recent years to strengthen its ability to conduct such activities. Among the most readily visible of the Navy's current IW operations are those being carried out by Navy sailors serving ashore in Afghanistan and Iraq. Many of the Navy's contributions to IW operations around the world are made by Navy individual augmentees (IAs)—individual Navy sailors assigned to various DOD operations.

The Navy Expeditionary Combat Command (NECC) was established informally in October 2005 and formally on January 13, 2006. The creation of NECC consolidated and facilitated the expansion of a number of Navy organizations that have a role in IW operations.

The Navy's riverine force is intended to supplement the riverine capabilities of the Navy's SEALs (the Navy's Sea-Air-Land special

---

[*] This is an edited, reformatted and augmented version of a Congressional Research Service publication, CRS Report for Congress RS22373, from www.crs.gov, dated April 11, 2011.

operations forces) and relieve Marines who had been conducting maritime security operations in ports and waterways in Iraq. The three current riverine squadrons were established in 2006-2007. The Navy's proposed FY20 11 budget requested funding for the establishment of a new reserve component riverine training squadron that is to complement the three existing active component riverine squadrons. The fourth riverine squadron is intended to increase the riverine capacity to conduct brown water training and partnership activities in order to meet combatant commander (COCOM) demands.

The Navy in July 2008 established the Navy Irregular Warfare Office, and in January 2010 published a vision statement for irregular warfare.

The Global Maritime Partnership is a U.S. Navy initiative to achieve an enhanced degree of cooperation between the U.S. Navy and foreign navies, coast guards, and maritime police forces, for the purpose of ensuring global maritime security against common threats. The Southern Partnership Station (SPS) and the Africa Partnership Station (APS) are Navy ships, such as amphibious ships or high-speed sealift ships, that have deployed to the Caribbean and to waters off Africa, respectively, to support U.S. Navy engagement with countries in those regions, particularly for purposes of building security partnerships with those countries and for increasing the capabilities of those countries for performing maritime-security operations.

The Navy's IW and CT activities pose a number of potential oversight issues for Congress, including the definition of Navy IW activities, specific Navy IW budget priorities, and how much emphasis to place on IW and CT activities in future Navy budgets.

INTRODUCTION

This report provides background information and potential issues for Congress on the Navy's irregular warfare (IW) and counterterrorism (CT) operations. The Navy's IW and CT activities pose a number of potential oversight issues for Congress, including the definition of Navy IW activities, specific Navy IW budget priorities, and how much emphasis to place on IW and CT activities in future Navy budgets. Congress' decisions regarding Navy IW and CT operations can affect Navy operations and funding requirements, and the implementation of the nation's overall IW and CT strategies.

Background[1]

Navy Irregular Warfare (IW) Operations

Shift in Terminology from IW to Confronting Irregular Challenges (CIC)

Use of the term irregular warfare has declined within DOD since 2010. DOD's report on the 2010 Quadrennial Defense Review, for example, avoids the term and instead uses the phrase counterinsurgency, stability, and counterterrorism operations. Consistent with DOD's declining use of the term irregular warfare, the Navy increasingly is using the phrase confronting irregular challenges (CIC) instead of the term irregular warfare. For purposes of convenience, this report continues to use the term irregular warfare and the abbreviation IW.

Navy Summary of Its IW Operations, Including Those in Afghanistan and Iraq

In summarizing the Navy's IW operations in Afghanistan and Iraq, Admiral Gary Roughead, the Chief of Naval Operations, stated on October 12, 2010, that:

> ...I want to be very clear, that we in the United States Navy, every Sailor, is fully committed to the operations and the fights that are being undertaken in Iraq and Afghanistan.
>
> It may come as a surprise to many that the United States Navy has 15,000 Sailors on the ground in Iraq and Afghanistan and in the Horn of Africa. That is 3,000 more Sailors that are serving that are on our ships in the Middle East. In fact, when you combined [sic] the 15,000 ashore and the roughly 12 or so thousand at sea, our presence in the Middle East is about the same as the United States Marine Corps. It has been that way for some time and it will continue along those lines. And even though the forces at sea may not be view[ed] as contributing toward the operations there and [sic: in fact] 30 percent of the fixed-wing aircraft that fly over our troops in Afghanistan are flying from the decks of the United States Navy aircraft carriers to support the ongoing operations there.[2]

The Department of the Navy (DON), which includes the Navy and Marine Corps, stated in early 2011 that:

Beyond the 20,000 participating in counterinsurgency, security cooperation, and civil- military operations in Afghanistan, on any given day there are approximately 12,000 Sailors ashore and another 10,000 afloat throughout U.S. Central Command (CENTCOM). These Sailors are conducting riverine operations, maritime infrastructure protection, explosive ordnance disposal, combat construction engineering, cargo handling, combat logistics, maritime security, customs inspections, detainee operations, civil affairs, base operations and other forward presence activities. In collaboration with the U.S. Coast Guard, the Navy also conducts critical port operations, port and oil platform security, and maritime interception operations. Included in our globally sourced forces are IAs [individual augmentees] serving in a variety of joint or coalition billets, either in the training pipeline or on station. As these operations unfold, the size and type of naval forces committed to them will likely evolve, thereby producing changes to the overall force posture of naval forces. Long after the significant land component presence is reduced, naval forces will remain forward.

While forward, acting as the lead element of our defense-in-depth, naval forces will be positioned for increased roles in combating terrorism. They will also be prepared to act in cooperation with an expanding set of international partners to provide humanitarian assistance and disaster response, as well as contribute to global maritime security. Expanded Maritime Interdiction Operations (EMIO) are authorized by the President and directed by the Secretary of Defense to intercept vessels identified to be transporting terrorists and/or terrorist-related materiel that poses an imminent threat to the United States and its allies.

Strike operations are conducted to damage or destroy objectives or selected enemy capabilities. Recent examples include simultaneous close air support missions that are integrated and synchronized with coalition ground forces to protect key infrastructure, deter and disrupt extremist operations or hostile activities, and provide oversight for reconstruction efforts in support of Operation Enduring Freedom (OEF) and Operation New Dawn (OND). Additionally, we have done small, precise attacks against terrorist cells and missile attacks against extremist sanctuaries. Among the various strike options, our sea-based platforms are unique and provide preeminent capabilities that will be maintained.

This versatility and lethality can be applied across the spectrum of operations, from destroying terrorist base camps and protecting friendly forces involved in sustained counterinsurgency or stability operations, to defeating enemy anti-access defenses in support of amphibious operations. We are refocusing this strategic capability more intensely in Afghanistan in an effort to counter the increasing threat of a well-armed anti-Coalition militia including Taliban, al Qaeda, criminal gangs, narcoterrorists, and any other antigovernment elements that threaten the peace and stability of Afghanistan. Our increased efforts to deter or defeat aggression and improve overall security and counter violent extremism and terrorist networks advance the interests of the U.S. and the security of the region. The FY 2012 contingency operations request supports sufficient capabilities to secure Afghanistan and prevent it from again becoming a haven for international terrorism and associated militant extremist movements.

The Navy has over 40,000 active and reserve sailors continually deployed in support of the contingency operations overseas serving as members of carrier strike groups, expeditionary strike groups, Special Operating Forces, Seabee units, Marine forces, medical units, and as IAs. Our Sailors and Marines are fully engaged on the ground, in the air, and at sea in support of operations in Iraq and Afghanistan. All forces should be withdrawn from OND by the end of 2011. Navy Commanders are leading seven of the thirteen U.S.-lead Provincial Reconstruction Teams in Afghanistan. A significant portion of the combat air missions over Afghanistan are flown by naval air forces. Our elite teams of Navy SEALs are heavily engaged in combat operations, Navy Explosive Ordnance Disposal (EOD) platoons are defusing IEDs and landmines. Our SEABEE construction battalions are rebuilding schools and restoring critical infrastructure. Navy sealift is delivering the majority of heavy war equipment to CENTCOM, while Navy logisticians are ensuring materiel arrives on time. Our Navy doctors are providing medical assistance in the field and at forward operating bases. Navy IAs are providing combat support and combat service support for Army and Marine Corps personnel in Iraq and Afghanistan. As IAs they are fulfilling vital roles by serving in traditional Navy roles such as USMC support, maritime and port security, cargo handling, airlift support, Seabee units, and as a member of joint task force/Combatant Commanders staffs. On the water, Navy Expeditionary Combat Command (NECC) Riverine forces are working closely with the Iraqi Navy to safeguard Iraqi infrastructure and provide maritime security in key waterways. Navy forces are also intercepting smugglers and insurgents and protecting Iraqi and partner nation oil and gas infrastructure. We know the sea lanes must remain open for the transit of oil, the lifeblood of the Iraqi economy, and our ships and sailor are making that happen.[3]

More specifically, the Navy states that operations performed by Navy personnel in Afghanistan and Iraq include or have included the following:

- **close air support (CAS) and airborne reconnaissance** operations, in which Navy aircraft have accounted for 30% of all such missions;
- **expeditionary electronic warfare** operations, including operations to defeat improvised explosive devices (IEDs), 75% of airborne electronic attack operations in Iraq, 100% of such operations in

Afghanistan, and operations to counter insurgent and extremist network communications;
- **intelligence and signals intelligence** operations, including operations to identify, map, and track extremist activity, and operations involving tactical intelligence support teams that are deployed with special operations forces (SOF);
- **explosive ordnance disposal (EOD)** operations, including defusing IEDs, clearing land mines, destroying captured weapon and explosive caches, and investigating blast scenes so as to obtain evidence for later prosecution;
- **riverine warfare** operations to secure waterways such as the Tigris and Euphrates rivers and the Haditha dam;
- **maritime security** operations, including operations to intercept smugglers and extremists going to Iraq and Kuwait, and operations to guard Iraqi and U.S. infrastructure, facilities, and supply lines, such as ports and oil and gas platforms and pipelines;
- **medical and dental** services in Afghanistan and Iraq provided by a total of more than 1,800 naval medical personnel;
- **logistics** operations, including transporting of 90% of military equipment for Afghanistan and Iraq on military sealift ships, operating ports in Iraq and Kuwait, and providing contracting services and reconstruction using Iraqi firms;
- **engineering and construction** operations, such as rebuilding schools, repairing roads, reconstructing electrical, water and sewer systems, and training and equipping Iraqi engineers;
- **provincial reconstruction** operations in Afghanistan and Iraq; and
- **legal** operations, including prosecution of special-group criminals and assisting Iraqis in drafting governing documents.

Navy IW Operations Other than Those in Afghanistan and Iraq

In addition to participating in U.S. military operations in Afghanistan and Iraq, the Navy states that its IW operations also include the following:

- **security force assistance operations**, in which forward-deployed Navy ships exercise and work with foreign navies, coast guards, and maritime police forces, so as to improve their abilities to conduct maritime security operations;
- **civic assistance operations**, in which forward-deployed Navy units, including Navy hospital ships, expeditionary medical teams, fleet

surgical teams, and naval construction units provide medical and construction services in foreign countries as a complement to other U.S. diplomatic and development activities in those countries;
- **disaster relief operations**, of which Navy forces have performed several in recent years; and
- **counter-piracy operations**, which have increased since 2008.[4]

The Navy states that enduring areas of focus for the Navy's role in IW include the following:

- **enhancing regional awareness**, which enables better planning, decision making, and operational agility;
- **building maritime partner capability and capacity**, so as to deny sanctuaries to violent extremists; and
- **outcome-based application of force**, so as to maintain continuous pressure on extremist groups and their supporting infrastructure.

Admiral Roughead stated on October 12, 2010, that:

> The multi-mission and irregular warfare capabilities we deliver in support of joint task forces in the Philippines and the horn of Africa, for example, directly support anti-terrorism efforts. Our counter-piracy operations in the Gulf of Aden have engendered unprecedented international cooperation at sea.
>
> Our demonstrated ability to partner with other agencies in the U.S. government, as well as public and private international organizations, have proven crucial in most effectively building partner capacity in Africa, South America, and the Pacific Rim.
>
> It is worth noting that the most recent Africa Partnership Station, an activity that is based on one of our amphibious ships in the most recent planning conference that was held in Naples, Italy, 25 nations came together to participate in that endeavor in preventative security and the rule of law. And since 2005, from our ships alone, we have treated over a half a million patients in Africa, Asia, Central and South America.
>
> Across such day-to-day engagement efforts to counter irregular challenges, naval forces preserve both the option and the capability to deliver decisive force in the event instability becomes disorder, but with the cumulative weight of established local relationships and political legitimacy in our favor.[5]

Navy Individual Augmentees (IAs)

Many of the Navy's contributions to irregular warfare operations around the world are made by Navy individual augmentees (IAs)—individual Navy sailors assigned to various DOD operations. DON states that:

> The Navy provides sailors in the form of IAs, including personnel in the training pipeline, to fulfill the OCO mission requirements of the Combatant Commanders (COCOMs). As IAs, they fulfill vital roles, serving in non-core missions such as provincial reconstruction teams, detainee operations, civil affairs, training teams, customs inspections, counter Improvised Explosive Device (IED), and combat support. IAs also support adaptive core and maritime missions including base operations, military police, combat support, counter IED, maritime and port security, airlift support, and Joint Task Force (JTF)/COCOM staff support. IAs are making a significant impact in more than 20 countries around the worldproviding COCOMS with mission-tailored, globally distributed forces. In FY 2012, the funding for 3,836 Navy non-core IAs has been shifted from the OCO budget to the base budget.[6]

Navy Counterterrorism (CT) Operations

Navy CT operations include the following:

- Tomahawk cruise missile attacks on suspected terrorist training camps and facilities, such as those reportedly conducted in Somalia on March 3 and May 1, 2008,[7] and those conducted in 1998 in response to the 1998 terrorist bombings of U.S. embassies in East Africa;[8]
- operations by Navy special operations forces, known as SEALs, that are directed against terrorists;[9]
- surveillance by Navy ships and aircraft of suspected terrorists overseas;
- maritime intercept operations (MIO) aimed at identifying and intercepting terrorists or weapons of mass destruction at sea, or potentially threatening ships or aircraft that are in or approaching U.S. territorial waters—an activity that includes Navy participation in the multilateral Proliferation Security Initiative (PSI);[10]
- working with the Coast Guard to build maritime domain awareness (MDA)—a real-time understanding of activities on the world's oceans;
- assisting the Coast Guard in port-security operations;[11]

- protection of forward-deployed Navy ships, an activity that was intensified following the terrorist attack on the Navy Aegis destroyer *Cole* (DDG-67) in October 2000 in the port of Aden, Yemen;[12]
- protection of domestic and overseas Navy bases and facilities;
- developing Global Maritime Intelligence Integration (GMII) as part of Joint Force Maritime Component Command (JFMCC) and Maritime Domain Awareness (MDA); and
- engaging with the U.S. Coast Guard to use the National Strategy for Maritime Security to more rapidly develop capabilities for Homeland Security, particularly in the area of MDA.

Navy IW and CT Initiatives

The Navy in recent years has implemented a number of initiatives intended to increase its IW and CT capabilities and activities, including those discussed below.

Navy Irregular Warfare Office
The Navy in July 2008 established the Navy Irregular Warfare Office, which is intended, in the Navy's words, to "institutionalize current ad hoc efforts in IW missions of counterterrorism and counterinsurgency and the supporting missions of information operations, intelligence operations, foreign internal defense and unconventional warfare as they apply to [CT] and [counterinsurgency]." The office works closely with U.S. Special Operations Command, and reports to the Deputy Chief of Naval Operations for information, plans, and strategy.[13]

Navy Vision Statement for Countering Irregular Challenges
The Navy in January 2010 published a vision statement for countering irregular challenges, which states in part:

> The U.S. Navy will meet irregular challenges through a flexible, agile, and broad array of multi-mission capabilities. We will emphasize Cooperative Security as part of a comprehensive government approach to mitigate the causes of insecurity and instability. We will operate in and from the maritime domain with joint and international partners to enhance regional security and stability, and to dissuade, deter, and when necessary, defeat irregular forces.[14]

The full text of the vision statement is reproduced in **Appendix B**.

Navy Community of Interest for Countering Irregular Challenges

The Navy in December 2010 established "a community of interest to develop and advance ideas, collaboration and advocacy related to confronting irregular challenges (CIC)." The community, which includes a number of Navy organizations, is to be the Navy's "standing authority to facilitate: implementation of the *U.S. Navy Vision for Confronting Irregular Challenges (Vision)*; promotion of increased understanding of confronting irregular challenges; and synchronization of CIC-related initiatives within the navy and with its external partners."[15]

Global Maritime Partnership

The Global Maritime Partnership, initially known as the 1,000-ship Navy concept, is a U.S. Navy initiative to achieve an enhanced degree of cooperation between the U.S. Navy and foreign navies, coast guards, and maritime police forces, for the purpose of ensuring global maritime security against common threats. The Navy states that

> The creation and maintenance of maritime security is essential to mitigating threats short of war, including piracy, terrorism, weapons proliferation, drug trafficking, and other illicit activities. Countering these threats far from our nation's shores protects the American homeland, enhances global stability and secures freedom of navigation for all nations. While our FY 2012 budget supports meeting this challenge, the future of maritime security depends more than ever on international cooperation and understanding. Piracy is an international problem and requires an international solution. The U. S. Navy will continue to function as part of a larger international endeavor combining efforts of governments, militaries and maritime industry to stop piracy on the high seas. The Navy remains engaged in counterpiracy operations, utilizing surface ships as well as long range P-3 Maritime Surveillance aircraft, as part of longstanding efforts to combat crime on the high seas. Disruptions to the global system of trade, finance, law, information, and immigration can produce cascading and harmful effects far from their sources. The increase in piracy off the Somali coast is a good example. The Navy is leading a multinational effort to patrol the waters near the Horn of Africa. A combined task force has been established to deter, disrupt and suppress piracy in support of United Nations Security Council Resolution 1851, protect the global maritime environment, enhance maritime security and secure freedom of navigation for all nations.

There is no one nation that can provide a solution to maritime security problems alone. A global maritime partnership is required that unites maritime forces, port operators, commercial shippers, and international, governmental and nongovernmental agencies to address our mutual concerns. This partnership increases all of our maritime capabilities, such as response time, agility and adaptability, and is purely voluntary, with no legal or encumbering ties. It is a free-form, self-organizing network of maritime partners – good neighbors interested in using the power of the sea to unite, rather than to divide.[16]

Partnership Stations

The Southern Partnership Station (SPS) and the Africa Partnership Station (APS) are Navy ships, such as amphibious ships or high-speed sealift ships, that have deployed to the Caribbean and to waters off Africa, respectively, to support U.S. Navy engagement with countries in those regions, particularly for purposes of building security partnerships with those countries, and for increasing the capabilities of those countries for performing maritime-security operations. The SPS and APS can be viewed as specific measures for promoting the above-discussed global maritime partnership. A July 2010 Government Accountability Office (GAO) report discusses the APS.[17]

Navy Expeditionary Combat Command (NECC)

The Navy Expeditionary Combat Command (NECC), headquartered at Naval Amphibious Base, Little Creek, VA, was established informally in October 2005 and formally on January 13, 2006. The creation of NECC consolidated and facilitated the expansion of a number of Navy organizations that have a role in IW operations. Navy functions supported by NECC include the following:

- riverine warfare;
- maritime civil affairs;
- expeditionary training;
- explosive ordnance disposal (EOD);
- expeditionary intelligence;
- naval construction (i.e., the naval construction brigades, aka CBs or "Seabee");
- maritime expeditionary security;
- expeditionary diving;
- combat camera;
- expeditionary logistics;

- guard battalion; and
- expeditionary combat readiness.

DON states that:

Navy Expeditionary Combat Command (NECC) is a global force provider of expeditionary combat service support and force protection capabilities to joint warfighting commanders, centrally managing the current and future readiness, resources, manning, training, and equipping of a scalable, self-sustaining and integrated expeditionary force of active and reserve sailors. Expeditionary sailors are deployed from around the globe in support of the new "Cooperative Strategy for 21st Century Seapower." NECC forces and capabilities are integral to executing the maritime strategy which is based on expanded core capabilities of maritime power: forward presence, deterrence, sea control, power projection, maritime security, humanitarian assistance and disaster relief. To enable these, NECC provides a full spectrum of operations, including effective waterborne and ashore anti-terrorism force protection; theater security cooperation and engagement; and humanitarian assistance and disaster relief. NECC is also a key element of the Navy's operational Irregular Warfare (IW) efforts in the area of operational support to the Navy forces in OIF and OEF.

NECC provides our most highly integrated force, smoothly combining active and reserve forces, highlighted by the seamlessly integrated operational forces of naval construction (Seabees), maritime expeditionary security (formerly coastal warfare), navy expeditionary logistics (Cargo Handling Battalions), and the remaining mission capabilities throughout the command. Beginning in FY2012 three Seabee Battalions and two Mobile Expeditionary Security Force Squadrons are converting from Active units to Reserve units.

NECC is not a standalone or combat force, but rather a force protection and combat service force of rapidly deployable mission specialists that fill the gaps in the joint battle space and compliment joint and coalition capabilities.[18]

DON also states that:

The Reserve Component expeditionary forces are integrated with the Active Component forces to provide a continuum of capabilities unique to the maritime environment within the NECC. Blending the AC and RC brings strength to the force and is an important part of the Navy's ability to carry out the Naval Maritime Strategy from blue water into green and brown water and in direct support of the Joint Force. The Navy Reserve trains and equips over half of the Sailors supporting NECC missions, including naval construction and explosive ordnance disposal in the CENTCOM AOR, as well as maritime expeditionary security, expeditionary logistics (cargo handling battalions), maritime civil affairs, expeditionary intelligence, and other mission capabilities seamlessly integrated with operational forces around the world.[19]

Riverine Force

The riverine force is intended to supplement the riverine capabilities of the Navy's SEALs (the Navy's Sea-Air-Land special operations forces) and relieve Marines who had been conducting maritime security operations in ports and waterways in Iraq. The riverine force currently consists of three active-duty squadrons of 12 boats each, and includes a total of about 900 sailors. The Navy established Riverine Group 1 (which oversees the three squadrons) at the Naval Amphibious Base, Little Creek, VA, in May 2006. The three current riverine squadrons were established in 2006-2007.

The Navy's proposed FY2011 budget requested funding for "the establishment of a new RC [reserve component] riverine training squadron which will compliment the three existing AC [active component] riverine squadrons. The fourth riverine squadron will increase the riverine capacity to conduct brown water training and partnership activities in order to meet COCOM demands."[20] The Navy stated that the creation of the fourth riverine squadron is to involve the realignment of 238 Full Time Support and Selected Reservist billets, and that the new squadron is to be the first-ever reserve component riverine training squadron within NECC.[21]

Other Organizational Initiatives

Other Navy initiatives in recent years for supporting IW and CT operations include establishing a reserve civil affairs battalion, a Navy Foreign Area Officer (FAO) community consisting of officers with specialized knowledge of foreign countries and regions, a maritime interception operation (MIO) intelligence exploitation pilot program, and an intelligence data-mining capability at the National Maritime Intelligence Center (NMIC).

Navy IW-Related Budget Initiatives

Discussion of IW-Related Programs in FY2012 DON Budget Highlights Book

In addition to passages quoted above, the FY2012 DON budget highlights books[22] states the following regarding elements of the proposed FY2012 DON budget that support Navy IW capabilities and operations:

The request [for FY2012 funds to cover the incremental costs of military operations] continues support for the fighting force in Afghanistan and the refurbishment costs associated with equipment returning from theater. Operational realities have maintained the demand signal for Departmental assets in theater for irregular capabilities as well as outside of the more traditional boots-on-the-ground support. ISR, airborne electronic attack, combat support missions flown from carrier decks with long transit times, and expanded counter- piracy missions are all areas that have shown persistent high demand signals from CENTCOM. (page 2-7)

The wide range of goods and services provided by NWCF [Navy Working Capital Fund] activities are crucial to the DON's conventional and irregular warfare capabilities as well as its ongoing roles in OCO [overseas contingency operations]. (page 6-8)

The FY 2012 budget continues investment in platforms and systems that maintain the advantage against future threats and across the full spectrum of operations. Procurement of the Littoral Combat Ship (LCS), Intelligence, Surveillance and Reconnaissance (ISR), Unmanned Aerial Vehicles (UAVs) and other programs that support irregular warfare and capacity building also continue to be emphasized. (page 5-1)

The Navy's shipbuilding budget increases since the FY 2011 FYDP and procures 55 battle force ships from FY 2012 to FY 2016 and one Oceanographic Research Ship. The budget funds a continuum of forces ranging from the covert Virginia class submarine, the multi- mission DDG-51 destroyer, the multi-role Landing Platform Dock (LPD 27), to the LCS and the Joint High Speed Vessel (JHSV) with its greater access to littoral areas. This balance continues to pace future threat capabilities while fully supporting current irregular warfare operations and supporting maritime security and stability operations in the littorals. (page 5- 2)

We continue to examine options for the LCS [Littoral Combat Ship] to help address emerging and ever evolving irregular threats. While naval forces are conducting combat and combat-support missions in Iraq and Afghanistan, the Navy and the Marine Corps also stand ready to answer our nation's call across the full spectrum of military operations through sustained pre-deployment training and enhanced Irregular Warfare (IW) training capabilities. (page 1-9)

Sustainment of the missions performed by the fatigued P-3 Orion fleet remains a priority for the Department. The P-8A Multi-Mission Maritime Aircraft (MMA), based on the Boeing 737 platform, begins replacing the P-3, with an Initial Operating Capability (IOC) in 2013. The P-8A's ability to perform undersea warfare, surface warfare and ISR missions make it a critical force multiplier for the joint task force commander. Additionally, the P-8A, which is authorized by the Defense Acquisition Board to have a Full Rate Production (FRP) award of eleven aircraft in FY 2012, will have increased capabilities over the P-3 as it addresses emerging technologies and ever evolving irregular threats. (page 5-9)

RDT&E, N [research, development, test and evaluation] initiatives support both traditional and irregular warfare demands in several aviation programs. (page 5-13)

The FY 2012 S&T [science and technology] portfolio [for DON] is aligned to support 13 discrete naval S&T focus areas composed of:... 4) asymmetric and irregular warfare.... (page 5-3 1)

Longer List of Navy IW Budget Initiatives

The Navy states that a longer list of Navy budget initiatives for creating or expanding its IW capabilities includes the following, which are not necessarily listed in any particular order of priority:

- shifting funding for the Naval Expeditionary Combat Command (or NECC—see "Navy Expeditionary Combat Command (NECC)" below) from the wartime operations part of the Navy's budget into the Navy's "base" budget (aka, the "regular" part of the Navy's budget);
- delivering expanded counter-IED and EOD capabilities;
- deploying riverine squadrons and maritime expeditionary support squadrons;
- training Navy personnel in foreign languages, regional affairs, and cultures;
- using the JFK Irregular Warfare Center at the Office of Navy Intelligence (ONI) to provide intelligence support to joint IW/SOF operations;
- ship operation and acquisition, including:
  - using ships (such as amphibious ships) as partnership stations, such as the Southern Partnership Station (SPS) and the Africa Partnership Station (APS) (see "Partnership Stations" below);
  - using ships (such as surface combatants and amphibious ships) for anti- piracy operations;
  - using hospital ships for humanitarian-assistance operations;
  - procuring Littoral Combat Ships (LCSs);
  - procuring Joint High Speed Vessels (JHSVs), which are high-speed sealift ships;
  - ending procurement of DDG- 1000 destroyers and restarting procurement of DDG-5 1 Aegis destroyers;[23]
  - operating four Trident submarines that have been converted into cruise missile and SOF-support submarines (SSGNs);[24]

- accelerating acquisition of the P-8 multi-mission aircraft (MMA), the Navy's intended successor to the P-3 maritime patrol aircraft;
- accelerating acquisition of certain unmanned systems, including:
  - the Navy Unmanned Combat Air System (N-UCAS—an unmanned aircraft that is to be flown form Navy aircraft carriers);
  - a sea-based, medium-range unmanned aerial vehicle (UAV);
  - the small tactical unmanned aerial system (STUAS);
- expanding the Navy's sea-based ballistic missile defense (BMD) capabilities;[25] and
- expanding the Navy's cyberwarfare operations force.

A separate list of Navy budgetary areas of emphasis for IW includes the following:

- ships and aircraft;
- persistent intelligence, surveillance, and reconnaissance (ISR) capabilities;
- unmanned systems;
- language skills, regional expertise, and cultural awareness (LREC);
- operations to build partnerships with other countries and to expand partner capacities;
- cybersecurity; and
- tools for fusing information from various sources.

In addition, the Navy states that with regard to rapidly fielding IW new capabilities, specific items of focus include the following:

- the Center for IW and Armed Groups (CIWAG)—an 18-month pilot project at the Naval War College in Newport, RI, whose current grant funding expires in June 2010;
- a large-diameter unmanned underwater vehicle (UUV) for ISR operations;
- Saber Focus—a land-based unmanned air system (UAS) that would be established in an overseas location and used for ISR to support IW operations;
- the use of ship-based Scan Eagle UAVs on converted Trident SSGNs for ISR operations;
- a surface ship- or submarine-based Maritime UAS that would be used for ISR operations and possibly signals intelligence operations;

- a naval intelligence fusion tool (NIFT) that is to integrate national and tactical ISR sensors so as to create real-time, actionable intelligence and targeting recommendations;
- a ship-based system called real time regional gateway (RTRG) for improved exploitation of signals intelligence to support IW operations; and
- an expansion in the size of helicopter squadrons that directly support special operations forces (SOF).

POTENTIAL OVERSIGHT ISSUES FOR CONGRESS

Definition of Navy IW Activities

Potential oversight questions for Congress regarding the definition of Navy IW activities include the following:

- Should security force assistance operations, civic assistance operations, disaster relief operations, and counter-piracy operations be included in the definition of Navy IW operations?
- Should operations to build partnerships, and to build partner capacities for conducting maritime security operations, be included in the definition of Navy IW operations?
- Has the Navy included the kinds of operations listed in the two previous points in its definition of Navy IW operations in part to satisfy a perceived requirement from the Office of the Secretary of Defense (OSD) to show that the Navy is devoting a certain portion of its personnel and budgets to irregular warfare?
- Should the Navy's CT operations be considered a part of its IW operations? What is the relationship between IW operations and CT operations?

Navy IW Budget Priorities

Potential oversight questions for Congress regarding Navy IW budget priorities include the following:

- Is the Navy's list of IW budget items sufficiently organized and prioritized to support congressional understanding and oversight, or to permit Congress to know where any additional dollars available for Navy IW operations might best be added?
- Should items such as expanding Navy sea-based BMD capabilities, procuring DDG-51 destroyers, and Navy cyber security operations be included in a list of Navy IW budgetary initiatives?
- Are the Navy's current IW-oriented UAV/UAS programs sufficiently coordinated?

Degree of Emphasis on IW and CT in Future Navy Budgets

A third oversight issue for Congress—an issue related to, but more general than the previous one—is how much emphasis to place on IW and CT activities in future Navy budgets.

Supporters of placing increased emphasis on IW and CT activities in future Navy budgets could argue that the experience of recent years, including U.S. operations in Afghanistan and Iraq, suggests that the United States in coming years will likely need to be able to conduct IW and CT operations, that the Navy has certain specialized or unique IW and CT capabilities that need to be supported as part of an effective overall U.S. IW or CT effort, and that there are programs relating to Navy IW and CT activities that could be funded at higher levels, if additional funding were made available.

Opponents of placing an increased emphasis on IW and CT activities in future Navy budgets could argue that these activities already receive adequate emphasis on Navy budgets, and that placing an increased emphasis on these activities could reduce the amount of funding available to the Navy for programs that support the Navy's role in acting, along with the Air Force, as a strategic reserve for the United States in countering improved Chinese maritime military forces and otherwise deterring and if necessary fighting in potential conventional inter-state conflicts

Potential oversight questions for Congress include the following:

- To what degree can or should Navy IW and CT activities be used to reduce the burden on other services for conducting such activities?
- Are the Navy's steps to increase its role in IW and CT partly motivated by concerns about its perceived relevance, or by a desire to secure a portion of IW and CT funding?

- Is the Navy striking an appropriate balance between IW and CT activities and other Navy concerns, such as preparing for a potential future challenge from improved Chinese maritime military forces?[26]

Additional Oversight Questions

In addition to the issues discussed above, the Navy's IW and CT activities pose some additional potential oversight issues for Congress, including the following:

- How many Navy personnel globally are involved in IW and CT activities, and where are they located? How much funding is the Navy expending each year on such activities?
- Is the Navy adequately managing its individual augmentee (IA) program?[27]
- Is the Navy devoting sufficient attention and resources to riverine warfare?[28]
- Aside from the establishment of the riverine force and a reserve civil affairs battalion, what implications might an expanded Navy role in IW and CT have for Navy force-structure requirements (i.e., the required size and composition of the Navy)?
- Is the Navy adequately coordinating its IW and CT activities and initiatives with other organizations, such as the Special Operations Command (SOCOM) and the Coast Guard?
- Are the Navy's recent IW and CT organizational changes appropriate? What other Navy organizational changes might be needed?

LEGISLATIVE ACTIVITY FOR FY2012

DON submitted its proposed FY2012 budget to Congress on February 14, 2011.

APPENDIX A. LEGISLATIVE ACTIVITY FOR FY2011

This appendix presents legislative activity (other than continuing resolutions) for FY2011.

FY2011 DOD Appropriations Bill (S. 3800)

Senate

The Senate Appropriations Committee, in its report (S.Rept. 111-295 of September 16, 2010) on S. 3800, recommends a $30 million reduction in the Operation and Maintenance, Navy (OMN), account line item for combat support forces, with the reduction being for unjustified growth in funding for NECC (page 31, line 1 C6C). The report also recommends transferring another $192.8 million requested for NECC in the same line item to Title IX of the bill, the title covering overseas deployments and other programs (page 31, line 1 C6C, and pages 207-208, line 1 C6C).

The report recommends a $4 million increase in the Procurement, Defense Wide account line item for Special Operations Forces (SOF) Combatant Craft, with the increase to be used for riverine special operations craft (page 1231, line 79); a $5 million increase in the Research, Development, Test and Evaluation, Navy (RDT&EN) line item for aviation survivability, with the request to be used for "AMTC Research and Development Riverine Command Boat" (page 150, line 27); and a $7 million reduction in the Other Procurement, Navy (OPN) account line item for standard boats, with the reduction being for an unjustified request for riverine patrol boats (pages 222-223, line 25).

FY2011 Defense Authorization Act (H.R. 6523/P.L. 111-383)

House (H.R. 5136)

The House Armed Services Committee, in its report (H.Rept. 111-491 of May 21, 2010) on the FY2011 defense authorization bill (H.R. 5136), recommends increasing the Navy's FY2011 request for operation and maintenance funding by $38.9 million for NECC integrated logistics overhaul and equipment reset. (Page 226, line 170)

The report states:

Navy Irregular Warfare and Counterterrorism Operations

Like the Army, the Navy's next-to-deploy forces are reporting high levels of readiness, but this also comes at the expense of the non-deployed forces that experience fewer training opportunities as resources are prioritized toward meeting Global Force Management demands. Navy requirements to support non-standard missions and requests for individual augmentees continue to grow, reducing opportunities for Navy sailors and officers to train for core missions with a full complement of personnel. (Page 220)

The report also states:

> The committee commends the Secretary of Defense for proposing to increase the authorized end strength of the active duty Army to 569,400 in the fiscal year 2011 budget request. The committee believes this effort will continue to assist the Army with managing of the force, increasing readiness and dwell time for soldiers. The committee also recognizes the Secretary's efforts to support an increase in the Air Force end strength in order to support its growth in Nuclear Enterprise, Irregular Warfare/Intelligence Surveillance and Reconnaissance, aircraft maintenance, acquisition, cyber warfare and medical fields, as well as the Navy's additional manpower requirements for 4,400 personnel to fill individual augmentees assigned to overseas contingency operations to execute non-traditional Navy missions, such as provisional reconstruction teams, detainee operations, civil affairs training, counter IED and combat support functions. However, the committee remains concerned that these increases may not be sufficient to meet both the increased operational tempo and the increasing support requirements that are being generated by a nation that has been at war for over eight years. (page 278)

Section 343 of H.R. 5136 as reported would extend by two years (from September 30, 2010, to September 30, 2012) authority to reimburse expenses for certain Navy mess operations. Regarding Section 343, the committee's report states:

> Section 343—Extension of Authority To Reimburse Expenses for Certain Navy Mess Operations This section would amend section 1014 of the Duncan Hunter National Defense Authorization Act for Fiscal Year 2009 (Public Law 110–417) by extending until September 30, 2012, the authority of the Navy to purchase meals on behalf of embarked members of non-governmental organizations, host and partner nations, joint services, and U.S. Government agencies and foreign national patients treated on Navy ships and their escorts during the Navy's execution of humanitarian and civic assistance missions. (Pages 274-275)

Senate (S. 3454)

The Senate Armed Services Committee, in its report (S.Rept. 111-201 of June 4, 2010) on the FY2011 defense authorization bill (S. 3454), states, in a discussion of amphibious ships, that Marine air-ground task forces are in high demand for certain missions, including, among others, irregular warfare, maritime security, humanitarian assistance and disaster relief, and security cooperation (page 38). The report states that the Navy's current 313-ship force structure plan

> is based on a 2005 Force Structure Assessment and a new Force Structure Assessment is required to address expanded requirements identified in the 2009 Quadrennial Defense Review for irregular warfare support, ballistic missile defense, intratheater lift, and humanitarian missions. The committee encourages the Navy to complete this review as expeditiously as possible so the results can be incorporated in the next Long-Range Plan. (Page 40)

The report also states:

Mobile Intelligence and Tracking Systems

The budget request included $117.9 million in PE 63114N [i.e., a line item in the Navy's research and development account] for advanced technologies for power projection. The Navy has a science and technology objective to develop data fusion and analysis technologies for actionable intelligence generation to defeat adaptive irregular threats in complex environments. In support of that objective, the committee recommends an increase of $2.0 million for research on data processing and fusion technologies to support multiple simultaneous detections, tracking, identification, and targeting of asymmetric and mobile threats in combat operations. (Page 60)

The report also states:

Autonomous Unmanned Surface Vehicle

The budget request included $45.9 million in PE 64755N [i.e., a line item in the Navy's research and development account] for ship self defense (detect and control) projects, but included no funding for the autonomous unmanned surface vehicle (AUSV) program. The AUSV program supports the U.S. Navy's anti-terrorism, force protection, and homeland defense missions. The AUSV can protect commercial harbors, coastal facilities such as commercial and military airports and nuclear power plants, inland waterways, and large lakes. The vessel will utilize a variety of advanced sensing and perimeter monitoring equipment for surveillance and detection of targets of interest. The committee recommends an increase of $5.7 million to continue this development. (Page 69)

The report also states:

West Africa Maritime Security Initiative
   The budget request includes $1,131.0 million for the Department of Defense's drug interdiction and counterdrug activities, of which more than $200.0 million will fund training activities for U.S. counternarcotics partners around the globe. The committee directs the Deputy Assistant Secretary of Defense for Counternarcotics and Global Threats and U.S. Africa Command to develop a West Africa maritime security initiative to include: (1) training in maritime domain awareness; (2) increasing the capacity of partners to patrol and enforce sovereignty in their own maritime space; and (3) improving the sustainability of their respective organizations with responsibility for maritime law enforcement. (Pages 199-200)

   Section 1011 of H.R. 5136 as reported would extend by five years (from September 30, 2010, to September 30, 2015) and clarify authority to reimburse expenses for certain Navy mess operations. Regarding Section 1011, the committee's report states:

Extension of Authority for Reimbursement of Expenses for Certain Navy Mess Operations (Sec. 1011)
   The committee recommends a provision that would extend section 1014 of the Duncan Hunter National Defense Authorization Act for Fiscal Year 2009 (Public Law 110–417), which authorizes the Department of Defense to fund from Navy operations and maintenance accounts the cost of meals on United States naval and naval auxiliary vessels for nonmilitary personnel, through September 30, 2015, and would establish an annual limit of no more than $1.0 million.
   In fiscal year 2009, the Department expended approximately $400,000 for meals sold to authorized personnel during U.S. civil-military operations, including Continuing Promise 2008/2009, African Partnership Station 2009, and Pacific Partnership Station 2009. The committee expects the Department's expenditures under this authority will increase in fiscal year 2010 due to Operation Unified Response/Joint Task Force-Haiti.
   The committee recognizes the value of recent civil-military operations and humanitarian relief missions—executed by the USNS

Comfort, USNS Mercy, and other vessels—and acknowledges the importance of building partnerships and fostering the positive image of America worldwide. The committee also understands that the participation of nongovernmental organizations and host and partner nations is vital to the successful execution of these missions. (Pages 187-188)

Final Version (H.R. 6523/P.L. 111-383)
Section 1021 of H.R. 6523/P.L. 111-383 of January 7, 2011, extends section 1014 of the FY2009 defense authorization act (P.L. 110-417), which authorizes DOD to fund from Navy operations and maintenance accounts the cost of meals on U.S. naval and naval auxiliary vessels for nonmilitary personnel, through September 30, 2015, and establishes an annual limit of no more than $1.0 million.

APPENDIX B. NAVY IRREGULAR WARFARE VISION STATEMENT

This appendix reproduces the Navy's January 2010 vision statement for irregular warfare.[29]

The U.S. Navy's Vision for Confronting Irregular Challenges

January 2010

CNO Foreword

Our Navy has a history of confronting *irregular challenges* at sea, in the littorals, and on shore. In the face of significant shifts in the nature and character of the threats our nation faces, this Navy Vision for Confronting Irregular Challenges will guide our efforts to prevent, limit, and interdict irregular threats and adversaries. We will focus on the full range of capabilities the Naval force can uniquely project, in and from the maritime domain, in countering *irregular challenges* associated with regional instability, insurgency, crime, and violent extremism.

The *Cooperative Strategy for 21st Century Seapower* places as much emphasis on preventing wars as it does on winning wars, and is the cornerstone of our approach to confronting *irregular challenges*. The six capabiNies of our Maritime Strategy, from winning the nation's wars to stabilizing regions with our partners, draws upon the cooperative and preventive capabilities of maritime and joint forces. Our Navy will realize the broadened and balanced capabilities directed in our Maritime Strategy and Defense guidance by making investments to ensure the agility, flexibility, and adaptability necessary to address the range of emergent challenges to our national security. We will enhance integration and interoperability with our traditional maritime partners, the U.S. Marine Corps and U.S. Coast Guard, along with other joint, interagency, private and non-governmental organizations. and international partners in all stages of this effort.

This Vision emphasizes the importance of the maritime contribution to addressing *irregular challenges* in a dynamic and evolving global security environment. The steps we take now will ensure our Navy is prepared fully to work with partners to stabilize regions at risk, and when necessary, dissuade, deter, and defeat irregular actors who seek to undermine security, stability, and prosperity.

G. Roughead
Admiral, U.S. Navy

I. The Vision for Confronting Irregular Challenges - Pursuing a Capability Balance for 21st Century Operations

> **Vision Statement**
>
> The U.S. Navy will meet irregular challenges through a flexible, agile, and broad array of multi-mission capabilities. We will emphasize Cooperative Security as part of a comprehensive government approach to mitigate the causes of insecurity and instability. We will operate in and from the maritime domain with joint and international partners to enhance regional security and stability, and to dissuade, deter, and when necessary, defeat irregular threats.

Recognizing the strategic impact of global threats associated with regional instability and insecurity, our Navy has instituted this Vision to guide efforts aimed at confronting *irregular challenges*. In today's interconnected and technically advanced world, **terrorists and criminals prey upon unstable and failing regions and pose an increasing threat to our national interests.** With three-quarters of the world's population, four-fifths of its capital cities, and almost all of its productive capacity located within 200 miles of a coastline, **our Navy is uniquely positioned and suited to counter threats to stability, while operating in and from the maritime domain.** This includes helping countries at risk build sustainable indigenous capacity to secure their resources, protect their populations, and stabilize their regions.

Our Navy must continue efforts to balance emphasis and investments between countering irregular threats and countering near peer forces to successfully meet today's and tomorrow's dynamic and interrelated security challenges. This Vision is derived from our Maritime Strategy and sets a course toward increasing proficiency in supporting direct and indirect approaches to dissuade and defeat *irregular challenges* -- wherein states and non-slate actors leverage uncontrolled or ungoverned space to employ informational, economic, technological, and kinetic methods against civilian populations and targets to achieve their objectives. **We will confront** *irregular challenges* **by focusing on the following outcomes:**

- **Increased effectiveness in stabilizing and strengthening regions,** by securing and leveraging the maritime domain, with and in support of national and international partners.

- **Enhanced regional awareness** of activities and dynamics to include a deeper understanding of ethnic, cultural, and socioeconomic characteristics and norms.
- **Increased regional partner capacity** for maritime security and domain awareness.
- **Expanded coordination and interoperability** with joint, interagency, and international partners.

These outcomes support promoting regional security and stability, advancing the rule of law, promoting good governance and prosperity, and help partners better protect their people and resources. They will inhibit the spread of violent extremism and its associated terrorist, insurgent, and criminal activities.

The Navy will leverage its history of presence, international engagement, and security enforcement, and will ensure our sailors, platforms, and systems are ready to address the hybrid nature of 21st Century challenges. The Navy brings global scope, unique access, and a breadth of capabilities to confront *irregular challenges*. We will promote Cooperative Security to mitigate instability in regions with limited governance that give rise to *irregular challenges*. We will enhance proficiency and effectiveness in security force assistance, maritime security, stability operations, information dominance, and other force applications necessary to support U.S. and partner counterinsurgency, counterterrorism, and foreign internal defense operations.

II. Opportunity: Leveraging the Maritime Domain to Confront Irregular Challenges

"Covering three-quarters of the planet, the oceans make neighbors of people around the world. They enable us to help friends in need and to confront and defeat aggression far from our shores."

A Cooperative Strategy for 21st Century Seapower

Our Navy's inherent contribution to the irregular contest is our capacity and ability to leverage access to the maritime domain and cooperate with partner navies and security forces to dissuade. deter, and defeat irregular threats at sea and ashore. While often overlooked in the context of *irregular challenges, the maritime domain enables proximate populations to partner and enhance their wealth and well-being, but also provides sanctuary and freedom of movement to criminals, terrorists, and insurgents.* The maritime domain provides for over 90% of the flow of information, people, goods, and services that sustain and create opportunities for regional economic prosperity. This economic opportunity promotes stability and helps prevent vulnerable populations from turning to terrorist or criminal enterprises.

The maritime domain similarly provides irregular actors with operating space and the ability to conduct the illicit flow of information, weapons, money, technicians, and cadres upon which much of their income and effectiveness relies. As such they are able to use the maritime environment to exploit, disrupt, or destabilize regions or governments, and to affect the will of civilian populations through insurgency, terrorism, crime, and the proliferation of radical ideologies.

The Navy's global maritime access and sustained presence forward enable U.S. Government-wide partnerships with nations and their forces to provide security and training assistance. At sea and ashore, the Navy works with partners to secure vulnerable maritime approaches and maritime resources, while improving collective capabilities to counter emerging threats such as piracy, trafficking, and weapons proliferation. Partners can appreciate the Navy's dependable but impermanent presence, which requires neither a footprint ashore nor infringement on their sovereignty. Our partners in turn add capability and capacity to our own through their contributions of forces, technologies, and operating concepts, as well as the understanding and ability to navigate local political, ethnic, and cultural contexts.

Today, the Navy is globally engaged to confront irregular challenges in sustained joint and interagency operations at sea and ashore. This includes support for counter-terrorist and counterinsurgency missions, development, humanitarian assistance, disaster response, and maritime security capacity building with partner militaries. Some examples include:

- Support for Joint Special Operations Task Force — Philippines which provides security force training, anti-terrorist forces, and delivered humanitarian relief and disaster response following storm induced flooding.
- Contributions to Joint Task Force — Horn of Africa whose East African Maritime Center of Excellence, security capacity building, and interagency policy efforts are enhancing indigenous capacities to stabilize the region and counter threats of piracy.
- Counter-piracy operations in the Gulf of Aden and the Horn of Africa which remove financial support to terrorists ashore and reduce instability and criminality at sea.

- Training and equipping partners for maritime security and fisheries enforcement in the Gulf of Guinea that many of the region's countries depend for economic stability.
- With coalition partners, the protection of oil platforms in the northern Arabian Gulf, that includes training for Iraqi naval personnel to assume this economically critical mission.
- Expeditionary Training Teams and Global Fleet Stations (Africa, South America, Pacific) dedicated to security force training and assistance through multi-mission employment of amphibious ships, tactical aircraft, and helicopters.
- The over 23,000 Navy personnel engaged in CENTCOM, with 14,000 ashore, conducting maritime security, river patrol, ordnance disposal, surveillance and reconnaissance, electronic warfare, and combat support operations, as well as providing non-naval augmentation for detainee affairs, security, and reconstruction.
- The procurement and employment of evolving multi-mission platforms oriented to lower end operations against *irregular challenges* including: Littoral Combat Ship mission modules, Riverine squadrons tailored for security force assistance, persistent manned and unmanned surveillance platforms, and investments in training capacity for language, cultural, and hybrid mission sets.
- The employment of multi-mission platforms able to work across the spectrum of conflict to include P-3 for surveillance against terrorists and insurgents, tactical aircraft for armed reconnaissance, and submarines and surface combatants in counter-drug operations.

The Navy will continue to pursue balanced approaches to confronting evolving irregular and conventional challenges by maximizing the multi-purpose effectiveness of our Navy's capabilities, personnel, and platforms. We will emphasize building partner capacity using dedicated training forces, periodic deployments and recurring exercises. In the end we will achieve the greatest effectiveness against the most likely 21' Century threats through an agile, flexible, and adaptable force.

These goals support the outcomes presented in this Vision:

- **Enhance and formalize interoperability** with U.S. government, public and private organizations, allied maritime and land forces, and regional partners.

- **Build partner capacity** by forming enduring, trust-based relationships, promoting shared interests in collective security, and providing training and resources to enhance indigenous security force capacity.
- **Improve our regional awareness and understanding of complex environments and challenges** through intelligence and information systems, training, education, and more culturally adept approaches.
- **Achieve an improved understanding and ability to counter illicit and extremist actors** as they leverage and maneuver in their maritime and shore environments.
- **Enhance and broaden the multi-mission capabilities and applications of today's force** to maximize effectiveness in complex regions and scenarios.
- **Identify necessary and distinct shifts in emphasis and investment to confront *irregular challenges*,** to include modifications to training, doctrine, and existing forces, and where necessary, new investments in processes, platforms, and systems.

In pursuing these goals for confronting *irregular challenges* the Navy will employ its broad capabilities to enable partners, improve maritime security, and conduct cooperative and decisive operations at sea and ashore. Specifically, we will operate to deny unregulated actors use of the maritime and littoral environment, assist in securing critical infrastructure to ensure the safe flow of resources, and apply a broad spectrum of maritime and overland capabilities to combat irregular threats while improving the lives of affected populations.

III. Implementing the Vision

Implementation will require a Navy-wide organizational approach. This effort demands changes in our thinking, our force and its preparation, and requires clear strategic communications within and outside the organization. We will comprehensively align our organizations, investments, procedures, doctrine, and training with the set of emerging approaches necessary to address these challenges.

Our Navy will pursue the outcomes and goals outlined in this Vision through these supporting implementation objectives.

1. Advance our Navy's doctrinal, strategic, and operational approaches to addressing *irregular challenges.*

- Increase our Navy's application of related Defense and Joint strategic and operational guidance.
- Define the strategic and operational tenets and approaches for our Navy to apply across our general purpose and special operation forces.
- Integrate the desired outcomes, priorities, and capabilities needed to confront *irregular challenges* into Navy's force development and management processes.

2. Organize, train, and equip our Navy to confront *irregular challenges* more effectively through balancing shifts in our investments and efforts.
- Enhance our ability to address, refine, validate, and incorporate urgent and emerging requirements to confront *irregular challenges* in the Planning, Programming, Budgeting, and Execution process.
- Identify the advocates and resource sponsors responsible for resource allocation and comprehensive program execution for existing and emerging Navy-unique and joint multi-mission capabilities to confront *irregular challenges*.
- Introduce the necessary supporting training and education requirements, to include organizations, curricula, and processes across our manpower enterprise.
- Institutionalize concepts, processes, and organizations for training and building the capacity of partners through dedicated assistance operations, regular exercises, and the deployments and visits of multi-mission ships and aircraft.

3. Emphasize interoperability and effectiveness for confronting *irregular challenges* across U.S. government, public, private, and international partners.
- Leverage Navy's multi-mission capabilities with other services, interagency and coalitions to build partner security capacity.
- Integrate and coordinate efforts with the U.S. Marine Corps and U.S. Coast Guard in support of the imperatives and approaches in the Maritime Strategy.
- Support the development of joint, interagency, and international operational concepts and supporting CONOPS.
- Support Defense efforts to integrate joint and interagency planning processes.
- Ensure capabilities to confront *irregular challenges* are addressed and captured in U.S. Navy and Defense legal policy development.

- Provide Combatant Commanders with applicable naval capabilities to support
critical mission requirements outside the scope of Navy core mission areas.

IV. Conclusion

Our Navy recognizes the importance of developing opportunities while being prepared to address irregular threats. Our general and special purpose forces are immediately applicable to the broad array of capabilities required to achieve regional security and stability. The Navy is uniquely positioned to assist emerging nations and fragile states, and to dissuade, deter, and when necessary, defeat irregular threats. We will build on our inherent strengths to lead and support national and international efforts.

The *Cooperative Strategy for 21st Century Seapower* places as much emphasis on preventing conflicts as on winning conflicts. This underscores the importance of securing and fostering long-term cooperative relationships based on mutual understanding and respect for each party's strategic interests, as well as increasing partners' ability to ensure their own security and stability. It recognizes the value of presence, of "being there," to maintain adequate levels of security and awareness across the maritime domain, and restrain the destabilizing activities of non-state actors. It makes clear our Navy will work alongside other U.S. services and agencies through a comprehensive government approach to advance international partnerships.

This Vision will guide and shape our Navy's actions, and will enhance our Navy's proficiency in capabilities to counter *irregular challenges,* now and in the future.

End Notes

[1] Unless otherwise indicated, information in this section is taken from a Navy briefing to CRS on July 31, 2009, on Navy IW activities and capabilities.

[2] Text of address of Admiral Gary Roughead, Chief of Naval Operations, at University of Chicago conference on terrorism and strategy, October 12, 2010, accessed October 22, 2010, at http://www.navy.mil/navydata/people/cno/ Roughead/Speech/101012-Uof Chicago remarks%20FINAL.doc.

[3] Department of the Navy, *Highlights of the Department of the Navy FY 2012 Budget*, February 2011, pp. 2-1 to 2-4.

[4] For more on counter-piracy operations, see CRS Report R40528, *Piracy off the Horn of Africa*, by Lauren Ploch et al.

[5] Text of address of Admiral Gary Roughead, Chief of Naval Operations, at University of Chicago conference on terrorism and strategy, October 12, 2010, accessed October 22, 2010, at http://www.navy.mil/navydata/people/cno/ Roughead/Speech/101012-UofChicago remarks%20FINAL.doc.

[6] Department of the Navy, *Highlights of the Department of the Navy FY 2012 Budget*, February 2011, pp. 1-10 and 1- 11.

[7] Edmund Sanders, "U.S. Missile Strike in Somalia Kills 6," *Los Angeles Times*, March 4, 2008; Stephanie McCrummen and Karen DeYoung, "U.S. Airstrike Kills Somali Accused of Links to Al-Qaeda," *Washington Post*, May 2, 2008: A12; Eric Schmitt and Jeffrey Gettleman, "Qaeda Leader Reported Killed In Somalia," *New York Times*, May 2, 2008.

[8] For a recent article on the 1998 strikes, see Pamela Hess, "Report: 1998 Strike Built bin Laden-Taliban Tie," *NavyTimes.com (Associated Press)*, August 22, 2008.

[9] SEAL is an acronym that stands for Sea, Air, and Land. Press reports in July 2010 stated that U.S. forces in Afghanistan include a special unit called Task Force 373, comprised of Navy SEALs and Army Delta Force personnel, whose mission is "the deactivation of top Taliban and terrorists by either killing or capturing them." (Matthias, et al, "US Elite Unit Could Create Political Fallout For Berlin," *Spiegel (Germany)*, July 26, 2010. See also C. J. Chivers, et al, "Inside the Fog Of War: Reports From The Ground In Afghanistan," *New York Times*, July 26, 2010: 1.) For further discussion of the SEALs, see CRS Report RS2 1048, *U.S. Special Operations Forces (SOF): Background and Issues for Congress*, by Andrew Feickert and Doc Livingston.

[10] For more on the PSI, see CRS Report RL34327, *Proliferation Security Initiative (PSI)*, by Mary Beth Nikitin.

[11] See, for example, Emelie Rutherford, "Navy's Maritime Domain Awareness System 'Up And Running'," *Defense Daily*, September 4, 2008; and Dan Taylor, "New Network Allows Navy To Track Thousands of Ships Worldwide," *Inside the Navy*, September 8, 2008. For more on the Coast Guard and port security, see CRS Report RL33383, *Terminal Operators and Their Role in U.S. Port and Maritime Security*, by John Frittelli and Jennifer E. Lake, and CRS Report RL33787, *Maritime Security: Potential Terrorist Attacks and Protection Priorities*, by Paul W. Parfomak and John Frittelli.

[12] For a discussion of the attack on the Cole, see CRS Report RS20721, *Terrorist Attack on USS Cole: Background and Issues for Congress*, by Raphael F. Perl and Ronald O'Rourke.

[13] Zachary M. Peterson, "New Navy Irregular Warfare Office Works to Address ISR Shortfall," *Inside the Navy*, September 1, 2008.

[14] Department of the Navy, Chief of Naval Operations, *The U.S. Navy's Vision for Confronting Irregular Challenges*, January 2010, p. 3.

[15] Source: Memorandum dated December 22, 2010, from S. M. Harris, Director, Navy Irregular Warfare Office, on the subject, "Confronting Irregular Challenges Community of Interest (COI) Charter." A copy of the memorandum was posted at InsideDefense.com (subscription required). For an article discussing the Navy's establishment of this community of interest, see Christopher J. Castelli, "Navy Taps Other Services, Elite Forces For Irregular Warfare Advice," *Inside the Navy*, January 17, 2011.

[16] Department of the Navy, *Highlights of the Department of the Navy FY 2012 Budget*, February 2011, pp. 1-5 and 1-6. For more on the Navy's contribution to multinational antipiracy operations near the Horn of Africa, see CRS Report R40528, *Piracy off the Horn of Africa*, by Lauren Ploch et al.

[17] Government Accountability Office, *Defense Management[:]Improved Planning, Training, and Interagency Collaboration Could Strengthen DOD's Efforts in Africa*, GAO-10-794, July 2010, 63 pp.

[18] Department of the Navy, *Highlights of the Department of the Navy FY 2012 Budget*, February 2011, p. 4-15.

[19] Department of the Navy, *Highlights of the Department of the Navy FY 2012 Budget*, February 2011, p. 4-25.

[20] Department of the Navy, *Highlights of the Department of the Navy FY 2011 Budget*, February 2010, p. 4-24.

[21] Department of the Navy, *Highlights of the Department of the Navy FY 2011 Budget*, February 2010, p. 3-7.

[22] Department of the Navy, *Highlights of the Department of the Navy FY 2012 Budget*, February 2011.

[23] For more on the ending of DDG-1000 procurement and the restart of DDG-51 procurement, see CRS Report RL32 109, *Navy DDG-51 and DDG-1000 Destroyer Programs: Background and Issues for Congress*, by Ronald O'Rourke.

[24] For more on the converted Trident submarines, see CRS Report RS2 1007, *Navy Trident Submarine Conversion (SSGN) Program: Background and Issues for Congress*, by Ronald O'Rourke.

[25] For more on the Navy's sea-based BMD capabilities, see CRS Report RL33745, *Navy Aegis Ballistic Missile Defense (BMD) Program: Background and Issues for Congress*, by Ronald O'Rourke.

[26] For additional discussion of this issue, see CRS Report RL33 153, *China Naval Modernization: Implications for U.S. Navy Capabilities—Background and Issues for Congress*, by Ronald O'Rourke.

[27] For a discussion of the Navy's management of the IA program, see Andrew Scutro, "Fleet Forces Takes Charge of IA Program," *NavyTimes.com*, July 7, 2008.

[28] For an article that discusses this question from a critical perspective, see Daniel A. Hancock, "The Navy's Not Serious About Riverine Warfare," *U.S. Naval Institute Proceedings*, January 2008: 14-19.

[29] Department of the Navy, Chief of Naval Operations, *The U.S. Navy's Vision for Confronting Irregular Challenges*, January 2010, 7 pp. (including the cover page).

In: The Death of Osama bin Laden ...
Editor: Raymond V. Donahue

ISBN: 978-1-61470-479-9
© 2011 Nova Science Publishers, Inc.

Chapter 5

SENSITIVE COVERT ACTION NOTIFICATIONS: OVERSIGHT OPTIONS FOR CONGRESS[*]

Alfred Cumming

SUMMARY

Legislation enacted in 1980 gave the executive branch authority to limit advance notification of especially sensitive covert actions to eight Members of Congress—the "Gang of Eight"—when the President determines that it is essential to limit prior notice in order to meet extraordinary circumstances affecting U.S. vital interests. In such cases, the executive branch is permitted by statute to limit notification to the chairmen and ranking minority members of the two congressional intelligence committees, the Speaker and minority leader of the House, and Senate majority and minority leaders, rather than to notify the full intelligence committees, as is required in cases involving covert actions determined to be less sensitive.

Congress, in approving this new procedure in 1980, during the Iran hostage crisis, said it intended to preserve operational secrecy in those "rare" cases involving especially sensitive covert actions while providing the President with advance consultation with the leaders in Congress and the leadership of the intelligence committees who have special expertise

---

[*] This is an edited, reformatted and augmented version of a Congressional Research Service publication, CRS Report for Congress R40691, from www.crs.gov, dated April 6, 2011.

and responsibility in intelligence matters. The intent appeared to some to be to provide the President, on a short-term basis, a greater degree of operational security as long as sensitive operations were underway. In 1991, in a further elaboration of congressional intent following the Iran-Contra Affair, congressional report language stated that limiting notification to the Gang of Eight should occur only in situations involving covert actions of such extraordinary sensitivity or risk to life that knowledge of such activity should be restricted to as few individuals as possible.

In its mark-up of H.R. 2701, the FY2010 Intelligence Authorization Act, the House Permanent Select Committee on Intelligence (HPSCI) replaced the Gang of Eight statutory provision, adopting in its place a statutory requirement that each of the intelligence committees establish written procedures as may be necessary to govern such notifications. According to committee report language, the adopted provision vests the authority to limit such briefings with the committees, rather than the President.

On July 8, 2009, the executive branch issued a Statement of Administration Policy (SAP) in which it stated that it strongly objected to the House Committee's action to replace the Gang of Eight statutory provision, and that the President's senior advisors would recommend that the President veto the FY2010 Intelligence Authorization Act if the committee's language was retained in the final bill.

The Senate Intelligence Committee, in its version of the FY2010 Intelligence Authorization Act, left unchanged the Gang of Eight statutory structure, but approved several changes that would tighten certain aspects of current covert action reporting requirements.

Ultimately, the House accepted the Senate's proposals, which the President signed into law as part of the FY2010 Intelligence Authorization Act (P.L. 111-259).

Both the House and Senate Intelligence Committees appeared not to make any further changes to the Gang of Eight notification procedure when both committees approved respective versions of the 2011 Intelligence Authorization Act (H.R. 754; S. 719).

This report describes the statutory provision authorizing Gang of Eight notifications, reviews the legislative history of the provision, and examines the impact of such notifications on congressional oversight.

REQUIREMENTS FOR NOTIFICATIONS OF SENSITIVE COVERT ACTIONS TO CONGRESS

Under current statute, the President generally is required keep the congressional intelligence committees fully and currently informed of all covert actions[1] and that any covert action[2] "finding"[3] shall be reported to the committees as soon as possible after such approval and before the initiation of the covert action authorized by the finding.

If, however, the President determines that it is essential to limit access to a covert action finding in order to "meet extraordinary circumstances affecting vital interests of the United States,"[4] then rather than providing advanced notification to the full congressional intelligence committees, as is generally required, the President may limit such notification to the "Gang of Eight," and any other congressional leaders he may choose to inform. The statute defines the "Gang of Eight" as being comprised of the chairmen and ranking members of the two congressional intelligence committees and the House and Senate majority and minority leadership.[5]

In addition to having to determine that vital interests are implicated, the President must comply with four additional statutory conditions in notifying the Gang of Eight. First, the President is required to provide a statement setting out the reasons for limiting notification to the Gang of Eight, rather than the full intelligence committees.[6] The two intelligence committee chairmen, both Gang of Eight Members, also must be provided signed copies of the covert action finding in question.[7] Third, the President is required to provide the Gang of Eight advance notice of the covert action in question.[8] And, lastly, Gang of Eight Members must be notified of any significant changes in a previously approved covert action, or any significant undertaking pursuant to a previously approved finding.[9]

In report language accompanying the 1980 enactment, Congress established its intent to preserve the secrecy necessary for very sensitive covert actions, while providing the President with a process for consulting in advance with congressional leaders, including the intelligence committee chairmen and ranking minority members, "who have special expertise and responsibility in intelligence matters."[10] Such consultation, according to Congress, would ensure strong oversight, while at the same time, "share the President's burden on difficult decisions concerning significant activities."[11]

In 1991, following the Iran-Contra Affair,[12] Intelligence Conference Committee Conferees more specifically stated that Gang of Eight notifications should be used only when "the President is faced with a covert action of such extraordinary sensitivity *or risk to life* that knowledge of the covert action should be restricted to as few individuals as possible."[13] Congressional Conferees also indicated that they expected the executive branch to hold itself to the same standard by similarly limiting knowledge of such sensitive covert actions within the executive.[14]

Changes to Gang of Eight Provisions

Congress approved several changes to the Gang of Eight notification procedures as part of the FY2010 Intelligence Authorization Act (P.L. 111-259). First, it required that a *written* statement now be provided outlining the reasons for a presidential decision to limit notification of a covert action or significant change or undertaking in a previously approved finding. Previously, such a statement was required, but there was no explicit requirement that it be written. Second, the President is now required no later than 180 days after such a statement of reasons for limiting access is submitted, to ensure that all members of the congressional intelligence committees are provided access to the finding or notification, or a statement of reasons, submitted to all committee members, as to why it remains essential to continue to limited notification. Finally, Congress required that the President now ensure that the Gang of Eight be notified in writing of any significant change in a previously approved covert action, and stipulated further that the president, in determining whether an activity constitutes a significant undertaking, shall consider whether the activity:

- involved significant risk of loss of life;
- requires an expansion of existing authorities, including authorities relating to research, development, or operations;
- results in the expenditure of significant funds or other resources;
- requires notification under section 504 [50 USCS § 414];
- gives rise to a significant risk of disclosing intelligence sources or methods;
- presents a reasonably foreseeable risk of serious damage to the diplomatic relations of the United States if such activity were disclosed without authorization.

The unclassified version of the FY2011 Intelligence Authorization Act, which the House and Senate Intelligence Committees approved in 2011, contained no further changes to the Gang of Eight notification procedure.[15]

WHEN PRIOR NOTICE TO THE GANG OF EIGHT IS WITHHELD

Although the statute requires that the President provide the Gang of Eight advance notice of certain covert actions, it also recognizes the President's constitutional authority to withhold such prior notice altogether by imposing certain additional conditions on the President should the decision be made to withhold. If prior notice is withheld, the President must "fully inform" the congressional intelligence committees[16] in a "timely fashion"[17] after the commencement of the covert action. The President also is required to provide a statement of the reasons for withholding prior notice to the Gang of Eight.[18] In other words, a decision by the executive branch to withhold prior notice from the Gang of Eight would appear to effectively prevent the executive branch from limiting an-after-the-fact notification to the Gang of Eight, even if the President had determined initially that the covert action in question warranted Gang of Eight treatment. Rather, barring prior notice to the Gang of Eight, the executive branch would then be required to inform the full intelligence committees of the covert action in "timely fashion." In doing so, Congress appeared to envision a covert action, the initiation of which would require a short-term period of heightened operational security.

CONGRESS SIGNALED ITS INTENT THAT THE GANG OF EIGHT WOULD DECIDE WHEN TO INFORM THE INTELLIGENCE COMMITTEES

During the Senate's 1980 debate of the Gang of Eight provision, congressional sponsors said their intent was that the Gang of Eight would reserve the right to determine the appropriate time to inform the full intelligence committees of the covert action of which they had been notified.[19]

The position of sponsors that the Gang of Eight would determine when to notify the full intelligence committees underscores the point that while the statute provides the President this limited notification option, it appears to be largely silent on what happens after the President exercises this particular option. Sponsors thus made it clear that they expected the intelligence committees to establish certain procedures to govern how the Gang of Eight was to notify the full intelligence committees. Senator Walter Huddleston, Senate floor manager for the legislation, said "the intent is that the full oversight committees will be fully informed at such time the eight leaders determine is appropriate. The committees will establish the procedures for the discharge of this responsibility."[20]

Senator Huddleston's comments referred to Sec. 501(c) of Title V of the National Security Act which stipulates that "The President and the congressional intelligence committees shall each establish such procedures as may be necessary to carry out the provisions of this title."

With regard to Sec. 501(c), Senate report language stated:

> The authority for procedures established by the Select Committees is based on the current practices of the committees in establishing their own rules. One or both committees may, for example, adopt procedures under which designated members are assigned responsibility on behalf of the committee to receive information in particular types of circumstances, such as when all members cannot attend a meeting or when certain highly sensitive information is involved.[21]

Congressional intent thus appeared to be that the collective membership of each intelligence committee, rather than the committee leadership, would develop such procedures.[22] Moreover, the rules that each committee have subsequently adopted, while they deal in detail as to how the committees are to conduct their business, do not appear to address any procedures that might guide Gang of Eight notifications generally. Rather, to the extent that any such procedures have been adopted, those procedures appear to have been put into place at the executive branch's insistence, according to congressional participants.[23]

CONGRESS APPROVED GANG OF EIGHT NOTIFICATIONS IN 1980, FOLLOWING THE IRAN HOSTAGE RESCUE ATTEMPT

Congress approved the Gang of Eight notification provision in 1980 as part of a broader package of statutory intelligence oversight measures generally aimed at tightening intelligence oversight while also providing the Central Intelligence Agency (CIA) greater leeway to carry out covert operations,[24] following a failed covert operation to rescue American embassy hostages in Iran.[25]

Congressional approval came after President Jimmy Carter decided not to notify the intelligence committees of the operation in advance because of concerns over operational security and the risk of disclosure. Director of Central Intelligence Stansfield Turner briefed the congressional intelligence committees only after the operations had been conducted. Although most members reportedly expressed their understanding of the demands for secrecy and thus the

Administration's decision to withhold prior notification,[26] Senate Intelligence Committee Chairman Birch Bayh expressed concern that the executive branch's action reflected a distrust of the committees. He suggested that future administrations could address disclosure concerns by notifying a more limited number of Members "so that at least somebody in the oversight mechanism would know.... If oversight is to function better, you first need it to function [at all]."[27] Such sentiments appear to have contributed to the subsequent decision by Congress to permit the executive branch to notify the Gang of Eight in such cases.[28]

AUTHORITY OF GANG OF EIGHT TO AFFECT COVERT ACTION

Even with statutory arrangements governing covert action, including Gang of Eight covert actions, Congress does not have the authority under statute to veto outright a covert action. Indeed, former Senator Howard Baker successfully pushed the inclusion in the 1980 legislative package of a provision making clear that Congress did not have approval authority over the initiation of any particular covert action.[29]

Nonetheless, the Gang of Eight Members, as do the intelligence committees, arguably have the authority to influence whether and how such covert actions are conducted over time. For example, Members could express opposition to the initiation of a particular covert action. Some observers assert that in the absence of Members' agreement to the initiation of the covert action involved, barring such agreement, an administration would have to think carefully before proceeding with such a covert action as planned.[30]

The Gang of Eight over time could also influence funding for such operations. Initial funding for a covert action generally comes from the CIA's Reserve for Contingency Fund, for which Congress provides an annual appropriation. Once appropriated, the CIA can fund a covert action using money from this fund, without having to seek congressional approval. But the executive branch generally must seek additional funds to replenish the reserve on an annual basis. If the Gang of Eight, including the two committee chairmen and ranking members, were to agree not to continue funding for a certain covert action, they arguably could impress on the membership of the two committees not to replenish the reserve fund, providing they informed the committees of the covert action, a decision which the congressional sponsors said they intended to be left to the discretion of the Gang of Eight in any case.
   Thus, the Gang of Eight could influence the intelligence committees to increase, decrease or eliminate authorized funding of a particular covert action. Some observers point out, however, that the leaders' overall effectiveness in influencing a particular covert action turns at least as much on their capability to conduct effective oversight of covert action as it does on their legal authority.

IMPACT ON CONGRESSIONAL INTELLIGENCE OVERSIGHT

   The impact of Gang of Eight notifications on the effectiveness of congressional intelligence oversight continues to be debated.
   Supporters of the Gang of Eight process contend that such notifications continue to serve their original purpose, which, they assert, is to protect operational security of particularly sensitive covert actions that involve vital U.S. interests while still involving Congress in oversight. Further, they point out that although Members receiving these notifications may be constrained in sharing detailed information about the notifications with other intelligence committee members and staff, these same Members can raise concerns directly with the President and the congressional leadership and thereby seek to have any concerns addressed.[31] Supporters also argue that Members receiving these restricted briefings have at their disposal a number of legislative remedies if they decide to oppose a particular covert action program, including the capability to use the appropriations process to withhold funding until the executive branch behaves according to Congress's will.[32]

Critics counter with the following points. First, they say, Gang of Eight notifications do not provide for effective congressional oversight because participating Members "cannot take notes, seek the advice of their counsel, or even discuss the issues raised with their committee colleagues."[33] Second, they contend that Gang of Eight notifications have been "overused."[34] Third, they assert that, in certain instances, the executive branch did not provide an opportunity to Gang of Eight Members to approve or disapprove of the program being briefed to them.[35] And fourth, they contend that the "limited information provided Congress was so overly restricted that it prevented members of Congress from conducting meaningful oversight."[36]

GANG OF EIGHT NOTIFICATIONS: THE HISTORIC RECORD

Notwithstanding the continuing debate over the merits of such notifications, what remains less clear is the historic record of compliance with Gang of Eight provisions set out in statute. Questions include: have such notifications generally been limited to covert actions, ones that conform to congressional intent that such covert actions be highly sensitive and involve the risk to life? When prior notification is limited to the Gang of Eight, has the executive branch provided an explanatory statement as to why it limited notification to the Gang of Eight? If the Gang of Eight is not provided prior notice, has the executive branch then informed the intelligence committees at a later date and provided a reason why prior notification was not provided? Has the Gang of Eight, once notified, ever then made a determination to notify the intelligence committees, a prerogative envisioned by its congressional sponsors? Have the congressional intelligence committees, at any time since they were established, attempted to develop procedures to guide Gang of Eight notifications, as envisioned by the sponsors of the Gang of Eight provision?

CONCLUSION: STRIKING A BALANCE

Striking the proper balance between effective oversight and security remains a challenge to Congress and the executive. Doing so in cases involving particularly sensitive covert actions presents a special challenge. Success turns on a number of factors, not the least of which is the degree of comity and trust that defines the relationship between the legislative and executive branches. More trust can lead to greater flexibility in notification procedures. When trust in the relationship is lacking, however, the legislative branch may see a need to tighten and make more precise the notification architecture, so as to assure what it views as being an appropriate flow of information, thus enabling effective oversight.

End Notes

[1] National Security Act as amended, Sec. 503 [50 U.S.C. 413b] (b) and (c).

[2] A covert action is defined in statute as an activity or activities of the United States Government to influence political, economic, or military conditions abroad, where it is intended that the role of the United States Government will not be apparent or acknowledged publicly. See the National Security Act of 1947, Sec. 503(e), 50 U.S.C. 413b(e).

[3] A Finding is a presidential determination that an activity is necessary to "support identifiable foreign policy objectives" and "is important to he national security of the Untied States." See Intelligence Authorization Act for FY1991, P.L. 102-88, Title VI, Sec. 602 (a) (2), 50 U.S.C. 413b (a).

[4] National Security Act of 1947 as amended, Sec. 503 [50 U.S.C. 413b] (c) (2). See Addendum A, Title V of the National Security Act as amended. The authorization for Gang of Eight notification also permits the President to notify "such other Member or Members of the congressional leadership as may be included by the President."

[5] Ibid.

[6] National Security Act of 1947 as amended, Sec. 503 [50 U.S.C. 413b] (c) (4). The statute does not explicitly specify whether such a statement should be in writing, nor specifically to whom such a statement should be provided.

[7] Ibid.

[8] National Security Act of 1947 as amended, Sec. 503 [50 U.S.C. 413b] (c) (2). The President must comply with these last two requirements—providing signed copies of the covert action and providing advance notification—when notifying the full committees of covert action operations that are determined to be less sensitive than "Gang of Eight" covert actions. Sec. 503 [50 U.S.C. 413b] (a) (1) requires a written finding unless immediate action by the U.S. is required and time does not permit preparation of a written finding. In the latter situation, a contemporaneous written record must be immediately reduced to a written finding as soon as possible within 48 hours.

[9] Ibid, (d).

[10] Addendum A, S.Rept. 96-730, 96th Cong., 2nd sess. (1980), p. 10. This report accompanied S. 2284, from which Title V of P.L. 96-450 is derived. Gang of Eight notification was included in a new Title V, Sec. 501, Sec. 501 (a) (1) added to the National Security Act of 1947 as amended by Sec. 407 (a) (3) of P.L. 96-450.

[11] Ibid.

[12] The Iran-Contra affair was a secret initiative by the administration of President Ronald Reagan in the 1980s to provide funds to the Nicaraguan Democratic Resistance from profits gained by selling arms to Iran. The purpose was at least two-fold: to financially support the

Nicaraguan Democratic Resistance and to secure the release of American hostages held by pro-Iranian groups in Lebanon.

[13] Joint Explanatory Statement of the Committee of Conference, accompanying Conf.Rept. 102-166, 102nd Congress, 1st sess. (1991), p. 28. The Joint Explanatory Statement accompanied H.R. 1455, the FY1991 Intelligence Authorization Act, which was subsequently signed into law (P.L. 102-88). The "risk to life" language is not repeated in statute.

[14] Ibid.

[15] H.R. 754 and S. 719, respectively.

[16] National Security Act of 1947 as amended, Sec. 503 [50 U.S.C. 413b] (c) (3).

[17] Ibid. What constitutes "timely fashion" was the subject of intense debate between the congressional intelligence committees and the executive branch during the consideration of the fiscal year 1991 Intelligence Authorization Act. At that time, House and Senate intelligence committee conferees noted that the executive branch had asserted that the President's constitutional authorities "permit the President to withhold notice of covert actions from the committees for as long as he deems necessary." The conferees disputed the President's assertion, claiming that the appropriate meaning of "timely fashion" is "within a few days." Specifically, conferees stated, "While the conferees recognize that they cannot foreclose by statute the possibility that the President may assert a constitutional basis for withholding notice of covert actions for periods longer than 'a few days,' they believe that the President's stated intention to act under the 'timely notice' requirement of existing law to make a notification 'within a few days' is the appropriate manner to proceed under this provision, and is consistent with what the conferees believe is its meaning and intent." The conference report included the text of a letter sent to the chairman of the House Intelligence Committee, in which President George H.W. Bush stated: "In those rare instances where prior notice is not provided, I anticipate that notice will be provided within a few days. Any withholding beyond this period will be based upon my assertion of authorities granted this office by the Constitution..." See H.Conf.Rept. 102-166, 102nd Cong., 1st sess., pp. 27-28 (1991). Despite President George H.W. Bush's refusal to commit to either "timely" notification as defined by Congress, or any notification at all, Robert M. Gates, President George H.W. Bush's nominee as Director of Central Intelligence, said he believed that non-notification should be withheld for no more than a few days at the most, and that he would contemplate resignation if it extended beyond that time period. See Congressional Quarterly Almanac, 102nd Cong., 1st sess., 1991, Vol. XLVII, p. 482.

[18] Ibid.

[19] See Addendum B, copy of the Senate debate as recorded in the Congressional Record, 96th Congress, 2nd Session, Volume 126—Part 20, September 17, 1980 to September 24, 1980. See p. 17693.

[20] Ibid, p. 17693.

[21] See addendum B, S.Rept. 96-730, 96th Cong, 2nd sess. See p. 13 of the report.

[22] Ibid, p. 12.

[23] Letter from Representative Jane Harman to President George W. Bush, January 4, 2006. Another example of the informality which sometimes informs the intelligence notification process involves so-called Gang of Four notifications. The Gang of Four consists of the chairmen of the congressional intelligence committees, the Vice Chairman of the Senate Intelligence Committee and the Ranking Member of the House Intelligence Committee. The executive branch frequently limits certain intelligence notifications to these four Members, sometimes including committee staff directors, even though neither statute, or committee rules, appear to make provision for such notifications.

[24] Congressional Quarterly Almanac, Vol. XXXVI, 1980, p. 66.

[25] There actually were two separate operations — both of which constituted covert actions, since neither was undertaken to collect intelligence — to rescue U.S. embassy personnel after Iranian "students" overran the U.S. Embassy in Tehran on Nov. 4, 1979. The failed operation involved an attempted airborne rescue of U.S. hostages which was aborted when three of the rescue helicopters experienced mechanical difficulties. A subsequent collision of one of the helicopters and a refueling plane left seven American rescuers dead. An earlier effort resulted in the successful extrication of six Americans who had been working at the U.S. embassy but had avoided capture by taking refuge in the residences of the Canadian ambassador and deputy chief of mission.

[26] At the time, the Hughes-Ryan Amendment of 1974 requiring that the executive branch report on Central Intelligence Agency covert operations to as many as eight congressional committees, including the intelligence committees, was still the law.

[27] See L. Britt Snider, *The Agency and the Hill, CIA's Relationship With Congress, 1946-2004*, (Washington, D.C.: Center For the Study of Intelligence, Central Intelligence Agency, 2008), p. 283.

[28] Ibid.

[29] National Security Act of 1947 as amended, Sec. 501[50 U.S.C. 413] (a) (2).

[30] L. Britt Snider, *The Agency and the Hill, CIA's Relationship With Congress, 1946-2004*, (Washington, D.C.: Center For the Study of Intelligence, Central Intelligence Agency, 2008), p. 311. See also Mike Soraghan, "Reyes Backs Pelosi On Intel Briefings," *The Hill*, May 1, 2009. House Intelligence Committee Ranking Member Peter Hoekstra reportedly stated that Members of Congress are able to challenge policies they disagree with. "This is nuts, this saying, 'I couldn't do anything,'" Hoekstra told the Hill, adding that he at least once complained to then President Bush and got a policy changed, according to the newspaper.

[31] See Congressional Quarterly transcript of press conference given by Representative Peter Hoekstra, December 21, 2005.

[32] See Tim Starks, "Pelosi Controversy Suggests Changes to Congressional Briefings Are Due," *Congressional Quarterly*, May 14, 2009.

[33] See letter from Representative Jane Harman to President George W. Bush, January 4, 2006, regarding the National Security Agency (NSA) electronic communications surveillance program, often referred to as the Terrorist Surveillance Program, or TSP.

[34] See Tim Starks, "Pelosi Controversy Suggests Changes to Congressional Briefings Are Due," *Congressional Quarterly*, May 14, 2009.

[35] Press release from Senator John D. (Jay) Rockefeller, December 19, 2005, commenting on the Terrorist Surveillance Program initiated by the George W. Bush Administration. As discussed earlier in this memorandum, under Sec. 501(a)(2), nothing in Title V "shall be construed as requiring the approval of the congressional intelligence committees as a condition precedent to the initiation of any significant anticipated intelligence activity.

[36] Ibid.

INDEX

#9

9/11, 2, 4, 5, 11, 12, 13, 24, 31, 33, 39, 49, 54, 72, 73, 75
9/11 Commission, 73

A

access, 71, 82, 92, 100, 110, 123, 124, 133, 134
accountability, 11
adaptability, 107, 121
advancement, 38
adverse weather, 85
advocacy, 106
Afghan insurgency, 11, 33, 44
Afghanistan, 1, 2, 4, 6, 7, 8, 15, 17, 18, 19, 20, 30, 40, 41, 42, 43, 44, 45, 46, 47, 49, 52, 53, 57, 58, 62, 63, 73, 75, 77, 87, 90, 97, 99, 100, 101, 102, 110, 114, 129
Africa, 46, 61, 62, 64, 78, 86, 98, 99, 103, 104, 106, 107, 111, 119, 124, 125, 128, 129, 130
agencies, 7, 16, 20, 21, 22, 24, 48, 49, 54, 55, 58, 61, 71, 76, 103, 107, 117, 128
aggression, 101, 123
agility, 103, 107, 121

Air Force, 42, 83, 84, 85, 88, 89, 93, 94, 114, 117
airports, 61, 118
Al Qaeda, 1, 4, 6, 10, 20, 26, 27, 31, 33, 34, 35, 36, 37, 38, 39, 40, 41, 42, 43, 44, 45, 46, 47, 48, 49, 50, 51, 52, 53, 56, 57, 58, 59, 62, 63, 64, 65, 66, 68, 69, 70, 71, 72, 73, 74, 75, 76, 77, 78, 79
Al Qaeda cells, 34, 45, 57
Algeria, 37, 57, 58, 59, 60, 77, 78
anger, 14, 16
appeasement, 49
appropriations, 138
Arab world, 40
Arabian Peninsula, 7, 35, 51, 52, 75
architect, 40
armed conflict, 27
armed groups, 17
arrest, 37, 46, 51, 59, 71
arrests, 8, 16, 51, 65
Asia, 29, 49, 103
assassination, 37, 42, 43, 51, 53, 54
assault, 41, 46, 75, 93
assessment, 7, 25, 26
assets, 8, 22, 55, 63, 74, 81, 85, 94, 110
authorities, 6, 9, 44, 54, 75, 76, 84, 134, 141
authority, 4, 5, 47, 54, 63, 82, 91, 106, 117, 119, 131, 132, 135, 136, 137, 138

autonomy, 8
awareness, 103, 104, 112, 119, 123, 126, 128
Ayman al Zawahiri, 8

B

background information, 98
backlash, 55
Balkans, 42
barriers, 52
base, 34, 41, 44, 47, 49, 51, 62, 100, 104, 111
Belgium, 88
beneficiaries, 71
benefits, 53, 91
Big Bang, 77
bilateral relationship, 68
blame, 18, 56
blogs, 27, 30
Boat, 86, 91, 116
bomb attack, 48, 71, 76
border control, 61
border security, 60
Britain, 53, 54, 58
brothers, 58
Burkina Faso, 78
Burundi, 62

C

campaigns, 56
candidates, 92
capacity building, 78, 110, 124
Capitol Hill, 11
Caribbean, 98, 107
CERN, 58
Chad, 59, 61, 78
chain of command, 6
challenges, 22, 23, 35, 37, 52, 56, 61, 69, 99, 103, 105, 106, 121, 122, 123, 124, 125, 126, 127, 128
chaos, 53
Chechens, 44

chemical, 41, 45
chemicals, 54
Chicago, 76, 128, 129
Chief of Staff, 85
China, 19, 130
CIA, 3, 6, 12, 54, 55, 74, 137, 138, 142
cities, 48, 65, 122
citizens, 14, 35, 52, 58, 59, 65, 70
citizenship, 73
climate, 20
CNN, 29, 45, 73, 74, 75
Coalition Support Fund, 29
Coast Guard, 100, 104, 105, 115, 121, 127, 129
coercion, 31
collaboration, 36, 55, 100, 106
community, 8, 20, 25, 28, 33, 35, 36, 37, 38, 39, 61, 65, 73, 83, 106, 109, 129
compatibility, 69
complement, 98, 103, 117
complexity, 7
compliance, 139
composition, 115
conference, 65, 67, 93, 103, 128, 129, 141, 142
conflict, 4, 18, 23, 27, 38, 39, 42, 49, 52, 57, 69, 70, 125
confrontation, 69
Congress, 2, 3, 4, 6, 11, 12, 24, 29, 31, 33, 65, 76, 81, 82, 83, 91, 92, 94, 97, 98, 113, 114, 115, 129, 130, 131, 133, 134, 135, 136, 137, 138, 139, 141, 142
consensus, 4, 47
consent, 5, 27
conspiracy, 14
Constitution, 141
construction, 40, 100, 101, 102, 103, 107, 108, 109
contingency, 86, 87, 101, 110, 117
conversations, 73
cooperation, 10, 11, 12, 13, 15, 27, 36, 47, 55, 56, 60, 68, 71, 98, 100, 103, 106, 108, 118
coordination, 31, 34, 74, 123

Index

corruption, 12, 51
cost, 87, 119, 120
counsel, 139
counterterrorism, 1, 2, 5, 9, 12, 20, 23, 24, 26, 31, 35, 36, 37, 50, 51, 54, 56, 60, 61, 65, 71, 73, 74, 75, 78, 81, 88, 91, 97, 98, 99, 105, 123
covering, 116
credentials, 57
crimes, 31
criminal gangs, 100
criminality, 124
criminals, 102, 122, 123
critical infrastructure, 101, 126
criticism, 13, 16
Cuba, 4, 51
cultural imperialism, 79
curricula, 127
cybersecurity, 112
cyberspace, 23

D

data processing, 118
deaths, 48, 58
decision makers, 72
decision-making process, 23
deficit, 50
degradation, 25
Delta, 54, 88, 129
democracy, 26, 39
democratization, 50
demonstrations, 26
Department of Defense, 6, 20, 30, 61, 81, 83, 91, 93, 94, 95, 119
Department of Homeland Security (DHS), 23, 25, 30
deployments, 81, 86, 90, 116, 125, 127
depth, 100
destruction, 26
detainees, 51
detection, 9, 119
detention, 4
deterrence, 5, 108
development assistance, 50, 61

diplomacy, 61
direct action, 85
directives, 89, 90
directors, 141
disaster, 74, 100, 103, 108, 113, 118, 124
disaster relief, 103, 108, 113, 118
disclosure, 137
disorder, 103
dissatisfaction, 69
dissidents, 42, 44
distribution, 20, 22
diversification, 73
Doha, 75
dominance, 123
downsizing, 92
drug trafficking, 106
drugs, 57

E

eavesdropping, 55
education, 126, 127
Egypt, 41, 62, 73, 79
elaboration, 132
electronic communications, 142
embassy, 46, 53, 59, 67, 137, 142
employees, 27, 59
employment, 125
encouragement, 52
enemies, 37, 47, 88
energy, 51
enforcement, 38, 123, 125
engineering, 100, 102
England, 85
environment, 23, 50, 52, 61, 63, 87, 106, 108, 121, 124, 126
environmental regulations, 82, 93
equipment, 83, 88, 89, 91, 101, 102, 110, 116, 119
Eritrea, 63
Eurasia, 79
Europe, 39, 40, 58, 71, 74, 85, 88
evidence, 9, 12, 14, 36, 49, 56, 65, 75, 102

execution, 6, 117, 120, 127
executive branch, 34, 131, 132, 134, 135, 136, 137, 138, 139, 140, 141, 142
Executive Order, 63, 73
exercise, 4, 51, 87, 93, 102
expenditures, 119
expertise, 8, 36, 86, 112, 131, 133
exploitation, 109, 113
explosives, 62
expulsion, 53, 68
extremist movements, 101
extremists, 25, 46, 57, 102

F

facilitators, 44
families, 76, 82, 92
family members, 51
fanaticism, 10
fear, 15, 25, 52, 57, 67
federal agency, 31
Federal Bureau of Investigation (FBI), 23, 24, 25, 30, 31, 36, 43, 54
federal government, 16
Federal Government, 64, 71
financial, 8, 11, 19, 36, 67, 79, 124
financial resources, 36, 67
financial support, 11, 79, 124
fiscal year 2009, 119
fisheries, 125
force, 4, 5, 23, 35, 41, 42, 45, 47, 55, 74, 81, 82, 84, 87, 88, 90, 92, 93, 94, 97, 100, 101, 102, 103, 106, 108, 109, 110, 112, 113, 115, 117, 118, 121, 123, 124, 125, 126, 127
foreign aid, 13
foreign assistance, 11, 12, 34
foreign language, 84, 111
foreign nationals, 58
foreign policy, 1, 14, 15, 20, 26, 61, 69, 140
Fort Hood, 54
forward presence, 85, 100, 108
France, 52, 57, 58, 60, 74, 75, 77

freedom, 26, 106, 123
funding, 12, 58, 65, 91, 98, 104, 109, 111, 112, 114, 115, 116, 118, 138
fundraising, 38
funds, 40, 42, 45, 57, 65, 82, 91, 110, 134, 138, 140
fusion, 113, 118

G

GAO, 107, 130
Germany, 58, 129
global security, 25, 34, 35, 121
God, 38
goods and services, 110
governance, 17, 38, 51, 61, 123
governments, 2, 39, 43, 57, 60, 68, 72, 77, 106, 124
gravity, 34
growth, 61, 90, 92, 116, 117
Guantanamo, 4, 51, 76
guidance, 7, 21, 22, 23, 34, 74, 121, 127
Guinea, 125

H

Haiti, 119
Hamas, 73, 79
harbors, 118
harmful effects, 106
Hezbollah, 79
homegrown terrorist, 24
homeland security, 25
host, 37, 42, 117, 120
hostilities, 4
hotel, 43, 66, 71
House, 3, 12, 29, 30, 31, 90, 93, 94, 116, 131, 132, 133, 135, 141, 142
human development, 61
human rights, 27, 78
humanitarian aid, 71
Hunter, 117, 119
hybrid, 123, 125

Index

I

ideology, 22, 26, 35, 37, 69
immigration, 106
income, 60, 124
independence, 7, 33, 36, 60
Independence, 67
India, 11, 14, 15, 29, 30, 46, 49, 75
individuals, 7, 24, 26, 28, 31, 34, 36, 38, 39, 57, 60, 62, 65, 70, 71, 78, 90, 132, 134
indoctrination, 34, 52
Indonesia, 65, 66, 67, 68, 71, 78, 79
industry, 106
infrastructure, 37, 51, 100, 101, 102, 103
initiation, 133, 135, 137, 142
insecurity, 71, 105, 122
inspections, 100, 104
insurgency, 15, 18, 19, 53, 65, 70, 75, 121, 124
integration, 121
intelligence, 3, 8, 10, 12, 13, 14, 16, 22, 25, 26, 31, 35, 36, 41, 45, 48, 49, 52, 54, 55, 58, 59, 61, 67, 76, 92, 102, 105, 107, 109, 111, 112, 113, 118, 126, 131, 132, 133, 134, 135, 136, 137, 138, 139, 141, 142
intelligence estimates, 41
interface, 86, 90
interference, 56, 60, 68
intermediaries, 24
international law, 27
international terrorism, 4, 101
interoperability, 88, 121, 123, 125, 127
intervention, 71
intimidation, 31
investments, 91, 110, 121, 122, 125, 126, 127
Iran, 46, 76, 131, 133, 136, 137, 140
Iraq, 37, 42, 53, 70, 82, 86, 90, 91, 95, 97, 98, 99, 101, 102, 109, 110, 114
Islam, 31, 38, 39, 50, 63, 64, 66, 68, 76, 79
Islamabad, 9, 10, 11, 12, 13, 15, 16, 29, 48, 49, 73, 74

Islamic law, 38, 69
Islamic state, 41, 57
Islamism, 39, 72
Israel, 41, 69
issues, 2, 9, 23, 24, 27, 37, 78, 82, 98, 115, 139
Italy, 58, 103

J

Japan, 85
jihad, 24, 31, 38, 39, 40, 41, 42, 47, 54, 57, 71, 72, 79
jihadist, 23, 24, 25, 31, 36, 39
Jordan, 44, 79
journalists, 47, 65
jurisdiction, 31
justification, 14, 15, 31, 34

K

Kenya, 44, 62
kidnapping, 57, 59
kill, 5, 6, 69, 71
kinetic methods, 122
Kuwait, 42, 46, 102

L

landscape, 25
language skills, 112
law enforcement, 25, 36, 61, 119
laws, 6
lead, 8, 23, 25, 54, 84, 91, 100, 101, 128, 140
leadership, 3, 5, 7, 8, 19, 21, 33, 34, 42, 45, 47, 55, 63, 64, 73, 75, 77, 78, 82, 92, 131, 133, 136, 138, 140
Lebanon, 76, 79, 141
legislation, 136
light, 14, 24, 26, 27, 65, 76, 85, 89
local government, 36, 39, 63
logistics, 61, 100, 102, 107, 108, 109, 116

M

majority, 76, 86, 101, 131, 133
management, 31, 127, 130
manpower, 62, 81, 86, 90, 117, 127
Marine Corps, 82, 83, 87, 92, 94, 99, 101, 110, 121, 127
maritime security, 98, 100, 101, 102, 106, 107, 108, 109, 110, 113, 118, 119, 123, 124, 125, 126
marriage, 11
mass, 53, 54, 85
mass media, 85
Mauritania, 57, 59, 60, 61, 77, 78
media, 10, 14, 47, 69
medical, 42, 71, 84, 86, 101, 102, 117
medical assistance, 101
messages, 39, 72
Mexico, 54
Middle East, 26, 28, 29, 30, 41, 56, 66, 73, 75, 77, 79, 99
militancy, 11, 14, 15, 49, 68, 71
militarization, 61
military, 2, 3, 4, 5, 6, 9, 10, 11, 12, 13, 15, 16, 17, 18, 20, 22, 27, 28, 29, 35, 42, 43, 45, 46, 48, 49, 50, 51, 54, 55, 56, 57, 58, 59, 60, 61, 67, 68, 70, 72, 81, 82, 83, 86, 88, 93, 94, 100, 102, 104, 110, 114, 115, 118, 119, 140
military aid, 56, 59, 60
military pressure, 18, 46
militia, 45, 63, 100
Minneapolis, 65, 78
minorities, 19
mission, 3, 6, 13, 16, 17, 20, 21, 22, 23, 24, 44, 86, 88, 89, 91, 92, 100, 101, 103, 104, 105, 108, 109, 110, 112, 122, 124, 125, 126, 127, 128, 129, 142
MMA, 110, 112
Morocco, 57, 77, 78
Muslims, 37, 38, 39, 40, 41, 46, 53, 68, 69, 70, 79

N

narratives, 26
National Defense Authorization Act, 91, 117, 119
National Intelligence Estimate, 47
national interests, 21, 122
national security, 2, 5, 20, 21, 34, 35, 37, 43, 121, 140
National Security Agency, 55, 142
National Security Council, 21, 30
nationalism, 15
NATO, 15, 17, 44, 45, 73, 74, 88, 94
natural disaster, 23
natural disasters, 23
NCTC, 7, 28, 78
negative effects, 47
Nigeria, 57, 60, 78, 79
North Africa, 26, 56, 60, 77
North America, 39, 64
Northwest Airlines, 76
NPR, 29
NSA, 142

O

Obama, 11, 12, 21, 27, 28, 30, 47, 48, 50, 54, 55, 68, 74, 79, 89
Obama Administration, 11, 12, 27, 28, 47, 48, 50, 54, 55, 74
officials, 4, 10, 11, 12, 14, 15, 17, 18, 26, 34, 41, 42, 43, 45, 46, 48, 49, 50, 51, 55, 56, 57, 60, 63, 64, 65, 70, 73, 75, 76, 78
oil, 52, 53, 60, 75, 100, 101, 102, 125
oil production, 52
online lectures, 54
Operation Enduring Freedom, 44, 49, 61, 87, 100
Osama Bin Laden, 27, 28, 30, 33, 34, 40, 46, 57, 62, 69
oversight, 6, 11, 34, 82, 83, 92, 98, 100, 113, 114, 115, 132, 133, 136, 137, 138, 139

P

Pacific, 85, 103, 119, 125
Pakistan, 1, 2, 6, 7, 8, 9, 10, 11, 12, 13, 14, 15, 16, 17, 18, 20, 27, 28, 29, 30, 34, 35, 40, 41, 45, 46, 47, 48, 49, 50, 52, 53, 57, 66, 73, 74, 75, 79
paralysis, 13
participants, 14, 60, 136
Pashtun, 15, 28
peace, 13, 15, 16, 64, 100
peacekeeping forces, 64
Pentagon, 29, 30, 73, 89, 95
permit, 4, 45, 114, 137, 140, 141
perpetrators, 15
personal relationship, 18
Philadelphia, 31
Philippines, 42, 103, 124
phobia, 52
piracy, 103, 106, 110, 111, 113, 124, 128
platform, 100, 110
poison, 58
police, 58, 59, 67, 68, 98, 102, 104, 106
policy, 2, 9, 12, 14, 17, 20, 26, 49, 68, 69, 124, 127, 142
policy issues, 2
policymakers, 5, 26, 56
political legitimacy, 103
political parties, 66
political party, 57
popular support, 71
population, 19, 51, 55, 76, 122
porous borders, 61
portfolio, 111
power plants, 118
precedent, 13, 142
predictability, 90
preparation, 31, 126, 140
President, 3, 4, 6, 9, 10, 15, 16, 17, 18, 21, 23, 27, 30, 41, 42, 45, 46, 47, 49, 51, 54, 56, 58, 62, 66, 67, 68, 73, 78, 79, 89, 100, 131, 132, 133, 134, 135, 136, 137, 138, 140, 141, 142

President Obama, 9, 10, 17, 21, 46, 49, 67, 68
principles, 38, 39
prisoners, 77
prisons, 67
productive capacity, 122
project, 36, 112, 121
proliferation, 63, 106, 124
propaganda, 69
prosperity, 121, 123, 124
protection, 16, 100, 105, 108, 118, 125
prototype, 91
public affairs, 73
public opinion, 50, 69

Q

questioning, 9, 11, 12

R

radicalization, 24
radicals, 57
reactions, 70
recommendations, 84, 87, 89, 113
reconciliation, 15, 18
reconstruction, 100, 102, 104, 117, 125
recruiting, 40, 71
Reform, 42
rehabilitation, 51
rehabilitation program, 51
reimburse, 117, 119
relatives, 56
relevance, 25, 114
relief, 108, 119, 124
reporters, 9
reputation, 37
requirements, 19, 23, 82, 84, 86, 87, 88, 90, 92, 98, 104, 115, 117, 118, 127, 128, 132, 140
resilience, 53
resistance, 14, 63
resolution, 78
resource allocation, 84, 127

150 Index

resources, 8, 20, 24, 34, 36, 41, 50, 61, 84, 86, 108, 115, 117, 122, 123, 124, 126, 134
response, 13, 25, 61, 67, 74, 77, 79, 100, 104, 107, 124
response time, 107
restrictions, 78
retaliation, 16
retribution, 25
rhetoric, 39, 57, 69, 70
rights, 19, 26, 27
risk, 93, 121, 122, 132, 134, 137, 139, 141
robberies, 67
root, 22
roots, 73
routes, 15
rule of law, 103, 123
rules, 136, 141
Russia, 19

S

safe haven, 11, 15, 17, 18, 20, 44, 47, 49, 51, 61, 62, 74
safe havens, 11, 15, 20, 47, 49, 61, 74
sanctuaries, 100, 103
SAP, 132
Saudi Arabia, 30, 37, 40, 41, 42, 43, 51, 54, 70, 75, 76
school, 71, 76, 101, 102
science, 111, 118
scope, 8, 17, 123, 128
scripts, 93
Secretary of Defense, 4, 49, 82, 83, 92, 100, 113, 117, 119
Secretary of Homeland Security, 36
security, 1, 2, 5, 7, 11, 13, 15, 16, 17, 19, 20, 22, 25, 26, 29, 33, 37, 47, 49, 50, 51, 52, 56, 57, 58, 60, 61, 62, 63, 65, 70, 76, 87, 98, 100, 101, 102, 103, 104, 105, 106, 107, 108, 109, 113, 114, 118, 121, 122, 123, 124, 125, 126, 127, 128, 129, 132, 135, 137, 138, 139

security assistance, 56
security forces, 22, 51, 56, 57, 58, 63, 65, 70, 71, 123
security services, 13, 15, 16, 62
seizure, 7
Senate, 3, 30, 31, 35, 36, 64, 72, 76, 78, 89, 90, 94, 116, 118, 131, 132, 133, 135, 136, 137, 141
sensing, 56, 119
sensitivity, 132, 134
sensors, 113
services, 10, 13, 16, 55, 81, 83, 102, 103, 114, 117, 124, 127, 128
Seychelles, 55
shape, 2, 15, 24, 38, 72, 128
Sharia, 63
Shiites, 76
shock, 16
shores, 106, 123
showing, 90
signals, 102, 110, 112, 113
signs, 13, 19, 37, 90
smuggling, 59
society, 14, 50, 66
solution, 18, 82, 106, 107
Somalia, 33, 43, 52, 62, 63, 64, 65, 71, 78, 104, 129
South America, 103, 125
South Asia, 28, 29, 30, 47, 49, 73
Southeast Asia, 65, 71, 78
sovereignty, 14, 16, 50, 119, 124
Soviet Union, 33, 41, 42
sowing, 53
Spain, 57, 58
specialists, 108
speculation, 10
speech, 17, 34, 72, 73
stability, 20, 61, 99, 100, 105, 106, 110, 121, 122, 123, 124, 125, 128
standardization, 88
state, 5, 9, 13, 23, 25, 32, 38, 47, 59, 60, 61, 65, 66, 67, 68, 74, 76, 81, 90, 114, 128
state control, 9

Index

states, 22, 23, 26, 50, 52, 54, 101, 102, 103, 104, 105, 106, 108, 109, 111, 112, 116, 117, 118, 119, 122, 128
statutory provisions, 4
strategic planning, 8
stress, 78, 82, 92
structure, 4, 27, 28, 33, 81, 87, 92, 94, 115, 118, 132
style, 58
submarines, 87, 91, 111, 125, 130
succession, 8
Sudan, 42, 62
Suharto, 66, 67
suicide, 44, 48, 58, 59, 62, 65, 74, 76, 79
suicide attacks, 58
suicide bombers, 58, 62, 65
Supreme Court, 27
surveillance, 13, 55, 104, 112, 119, 125, 142
survival, 16
sustainability, 119
sympathy, 14, 47
synchronization, 106

T

tactics, 17, 38, 51, 58, 71, 88, 94
takeover, 62
Taliban, 4, 10, 12, 15, 16, 18, 19, 30, 43, 44, 46, 48, 53, 73, 100, 129
Tanzania, 44, 62
target, 4, 5, 16, 48, 51, 53, 70, 75, 76
teachers, 65
teams, 55, 84, 89, 94, 101, 102, 104, 117
techniques, 88, 93
technologies, 111, 118
technology, 62, 111, 118
tensions, 15, 49
territorial, 104
territory, 10, 13, 14, 16, 27, 40, 46, 50, 53, 63, 77, 79, 83
terrorism, 10, 14, 15, 20, 22, 23, 24, 25, 28, 31, 49, 51, 52, 57, 60, 61, 63, 67, 72, 75, 76, 91, 100, 103, 106, 108, 118, 124, 128, 129

terrorist activities, 31, 41, 62
terrorist acts, 31
terrorist groups, 14, 17, 35, 36, 46, 61, 65, 67, 73
terrorist organization, 5, 28, 33, 37, 47, 61, 62, 66
terrorists, 2, 12, 14, 15, 23, 46, 47, 49, 54, 56, 57, 58, 61, 76, 88, 100, 104, 122, 123, 124, 125, 129
Third World, 70
threats, 20, 21, 24, 25, 26, 35, 47, 48, 49, 57, 60, 61, 62, 66, 70, 71, 86, 98, 106, 110, 111, 118, 121, 122, 123, 124, 125, 126, 128
Title I, 116
Title V, 136, 140, 142
trade, 106
traditions, 66
trafficking, 57, 60, 61, 124
training, 18, 33, 34, 36, 42, 44, 46, 53, 57, 59, 61, 64, 66, 82, 83, 84, 85, 87, 88, 90, 91, 92, 98, 100, 102, 104, 107, 108, 109, 110, 111, 117, 119, 124, 125, 126, 127
trajectory, 34
transcripts, 30, 95
transparency, 12
transport, 93
Treasury, 73, 75, 77
treatment, 135
tribesmen, 53
Turkey, 79

U

U.N. Security Council, 78
U.S. assistance, 9, 11, 29
U.S. policy, 2, 5, 6, 7, 9, 15, 17, 19, 27, 50, 56, 60, 61
U.S. Treasury, 74, 77, 84
unification, 51
United Nations, 62, 71, 106
United States (USA), 1, 3, 4, 5, 6, 9, 11, 12, 13, 14, 17, 18, 19, 21, 23, 24, 26, 27, 30, 31, 34, 35, 36, 39, 40, 41, 42,

43, 44, 45, 47, 49, 50, 52, 54, 56, 57, 58, 62, 63, 64, 65, 70, 71, 72, 73, 74, 76, 78, 93, 94, 99, 100, 114, 119, 133, 134, 140
Unmanned Aerial Vehicles, 110
uranium, 59
USS Cole, 129
Uzbekistan, 44

V

vehicles, 58
versatility, 100
vessels, 100, 119, 120
veto, 132, 137
violence, 31, 34, 39, 53, 54
violent extremist, 20, 21, 22, 103
vision, 26, 37, 98, 105, 106, 120

W

war, 4, 6, 14, 15, 21, 27, 28, 40, 41, 42, 49, 50, 57, 59, 60, 62, 101, 106, 117
Washington, 9, 11, 15, 27, 28, 29, 30, 52, 74, 76, 77, 79, 95, 129, 142
waterways, 98, 101, 102, 109, 118
Waziristan, 16, 49
wealth, 60, 123
weapons, 5, 20, 23, 34, 45, 51, 104, 106, 124
weapons of mass destruction, 5, 20, 23, 104
West Africa, 58, 119
Western countries, 49
White House, 22, 26, 27, 28, 30, 32, 55, 77
withdrawal, 15, 17, 19, 42
witnesses, 29
WMD, 5
workers, 53, 58, 59, 65, 77
World Trade Center, 42, 43
worldwide, 81, 87, 88, 120

Y

Yemen, 33, 43, 44, 46, 47, 51, 53, 54, 55, 56, 74, 75, 76, 77, 105